Ancient Footsteps:
The History, Mystery and Magic
of the
Isle of Portland

By
Scott Irvine

*This book is dedicated to my uncle and aunty, Portlanders, born and bred.
Pump Saunders, 1932–2022
Sandra Saunders, 1939–2022*

All rights reserved, no part of this publication may be reproduced or transmitted by any means whatsoever without the prior permission of the publisher.

Text © Scott Irvine

Edited by Toni Glitz
glitzedit.co.uk

Photography © Scott Irvine
Additional artwork
© Chloe Pasquale

ISBN: 978-1-916756-35-9

September 2025
VENEFICIA PUBLICATIONS UK
veneficiapublications.com

CONTENTS

INTRODUCTION i

WALK ONE: THE COASTAL PATH 1

NEWGROUND TO CHURCH OPE COVE.. 1

CHURCH OPE COVE TO PORTLAND BILL 28

PORTLAND BILL TO TOUT QUARRY.................................... 47

TOUT QUARRY TO CASTLETOWN 61

CASTLETOWN TO NEWGROUND 85

WALK TWO: CHURCH OPE COVE TO TOUT QUARRY ... 93

WALK THREE: CHURCH OPE COVE TO EASTON. 110

WALK FOUR: EASTON TO ST. GEORGE'S CHURCH 118

WALK FIVE: EASTON TO NEWGROUND 126

WALK SIX: CHESIL BEACH TO HALLELUJAH BAY 132

PORTLAND: A ROYAL MANOR 136

REFERENCES 3

INTRODUCTION

The island of Portland has a rich and varied history, from the Mesolithic Era up to the modern day, ripe with ancient myths and legends.

Its once-sacred landscape held high status as a royal manor before the Victorians turned the island into a huge defence project and opened the way for extensive quarrying across most of Tophill.

This book is a guide to the most interesting walks on the island, filled with tales from the people who lived and roamed here. My name is Scott and I am a Volunteer Coastal Ranger. It's my pleasure to take you on a journey around this sacred isle. In addition to my own experiences and memories going back to my childhood, this book contains many words from an interview recorded on 19th September 2012, with my late uncle, Pump Saunders, who passed away in 2022. Pump was a Portland quarryman for most of his life and was a wealth of information about his beloved isle.

In this book you will find tales of witchcraft and pixies, floods, shipwrecks and sea monsters, the Admiralty and spies, romance and deception, mysteries and corpses, destruction and innovation, and invasion and community spirit.

It is about the many quarries which have been methodically hewn from the sacred landscape for nearly four centuries, the practice of which continues to this day and shows no sign of abating. It is about the impact of the thousands of new builds, many taken up as holiday and second homes, from the legacy of the Olympic Games putting 'Portland on the map'.

The walks start at the top of the island looking down over Underhill and across to the mainland, with Chesil Beach at its most magnificent, stretching miles into the distance. It is a sight to behold whatever the weather.

You are then taken across the island towards the east cliffs, pausing in places to explore sites along the way. Reaching the coast, you are at the point where the full force of the elements come in from the Channel.

It is a dramatic windswept landscape dominated with stone spoil at the bottom of the cliffs.

We follow the coastal trail that is part of the South West Coastal Path, taking in the Admiralty defences, and southwards past the secluded Church Ope Cove to Portland Bill. We then head north along the west cliff past the old Admiralty base, now a business park and main school, to Tout Quarry Sculpture Park. The coastal path then journeys through Underhill and Chiswell to Portland Castle and along the old Merchants Railway back up to Newground, where we started.

There are four shorter inland tours going through Weston and

Easton, and a final walk to the serene and calm Hallelujah Bay below West Weares.

There is something for everyone; the main thing is to enjoy the adventure.

Welcome to Portland. Turn your phones off and allow me to take you on an adventure of mystery, intrigue and wonder.

WALK ONE: THE COASTAL PATH

NEWGROUND TO CHURCH OPE COVE

A good place to start this walk is Newground, just off the roundabout at the top of the hill, opposite the Heights Hotel. The car park is still free at the time of writing but there is talk that Dorset Council want to charge for it in the future. This is an ideal place to start and end, with coffee and snacks available at the hotel and a toilet nearby, next to the communications mast. It also has magnificent views to the north over Underhill and across to the mainland.

Now would be a good time to mention a dreaded word which we do not use on Portland. We have bunnies, coneys, underground mutton or long ears, but we do not ever use the 'R' word to describe them. For true Portlanders, that name is a curse word which brings bad luck when spoken aloud. Quarrymen once blamed bunnies for causing rock falls in the quarries, injuring many workers. If a quarryman saw a bunny on the way to work, he would turn around and go home for the rest of the day. I have instilled in my genes the folly of speaking the word from three generations of strong women.

R****t, a noun, a gregarious burrowing plant-eating animal with long ears, muscular hind legs and a short bobby tail. The Romans first bought the bunny to England as a simple nourishing meal. Known in Latin as a cuniculus, from the Greek 'kyniklos' which roughly translates as 'underground dog'. The Normans introduced the bunny mainly for hunting, allowing them to breed wild in the forests. They became known as 'rabet', from the French-speaking southern Walloon province of Belgium 'robete' from the word 'robbe' or robber, for stealing crops in the fields.

It is different today with many Portlanders owning bunnies as pets but many still consider the 'R' word to be unlucky.

From the car park, walk back towards the Heights Hotel, past the Olympic Rings sculpture, made by

Albion Stone from Portland Whitbed for the 2012 Olympic Games. It was situated at the entrance to Weymouth train station before being returned to Portland once the games were over.

Head to the fire beacon overlooking Priory Corner. The beacon represents liberation, a political separation from our neighbours across the way – Weymouth. Portland had been doing well for itself until the government decided to merge the two councils together, forming Weymouth & Portland Borough Council (WPBC) in 1975. For a start, Portland's name should have come first. It was not good for the islanders, with the ratio of councillors in the new administrative power stacked in Weymouth's favour, meaning that Portland lost out in every vote when it involved the island.

The beacon was constructed in 2019 to celebrate the parting of the two councils when all of Middle and West Dorset merged into one superpower, Dorset Council, on April 1st. The beacon was lit and attended by many locals, with talks from councillors, music and a burger van. To coincide with this, another beacon was lit across the harbour at Nothe Fort in

Weymouth, celebrating the same thing, albeit from the point of view of ridding themselves of their poorer cousins.

All I can say now is, be careful what you wish for.

The Saxon Charter of King Aethelred recorded in 867, mentioned the island called Portelond as one of his royal manors. The official meaning of the name Portland, according to academics, is land with a port, which at a glance might seem obvious but when looked at in greater depth, actually makes no sense. The harbour was not constructed until the late 19th Century. Before then, the safe and calm waters were called the Roads. They sheltered ships from the regular storms from the southwest, protected by the Chesil bank, but it was by no means a port. A trading post, yes, but not a port. Port is Latin, meaning passage or gate. The Romans called it the island Vindelis, which means windy isle, and if you have lived here as long as I have, you will know they named it well.

One of the first Saxons to arrive on our shores after the Romans left was Porteus, who made himself king of this island alongside, Portesham, a small fishing village at the other end of the

Fleet that separates the beach from the mainland. Porteus is credited for giving the island its name. Having control of both ends of Chesil Beach, the king would own the fishing rights in the Fleet and off the beach and all the salvage that washed up anywhere along it.

The importance of the sacred island is evident, as it is the first Dorset entry in the Domesday Book, completed in 1085.

> *'The King holds the Island called Porteland. It contains an area for his own use containing one manager, five farm workers and three ploughing fields. There are 100 smallholders with less than ten having twenty-three ploughing fields between them. There are eight acres of meadow and pasture land measuring eight furlongs square containing three work horses, fourteen cattle, twenty-seven pigs and 900 sheep. With what this Manor has in value, it pays taxes of £65.'*

Take some time to admire the view from here. Below us is Underhill, consisting of Fortuneswell immediately below, Verne Common to the right and Chiswell below them. Chiswell is Portland's second oldest village, established as a fishing community in the 17th Century, in the shadow of Chesil Beach.

The pebble beach was formed around 7,000 years ago at the end of the last Ice Age, stretching 18 miles to West Bay further along the coast soon after Portland became an island.

In 840, just over 50 years after the Vikings first visited the island, a full invasion force of 33 ships arrived.

Portland was already on alert after the same force had attempted to set up a bridgehead at Southampton weeks earlier. They were pushed back by Ealdorman Wulfheard – Ealdorman meaning noble chief, usually a prince ruling over an area of land – and retreated back out to sea.

In what was to become known as the Battle of Portland, the Vikings were met by the full force of Ealdorman Aethelhiem and his army lying in wait for them to arrive. After a long and bloody battle, the Saxons were defeated and the island taken. Aethelhiem was killed in battle alongside many of his men. The story from the Anglo Saxon Chronicles reports that the battle occurred at the north of the island, around Chiswell area. There is a small green oasis surrounded by houses inland from the Cove Inn on the sea wall. It is an ancient burial mound called Mound Oel, Owl or Howell. It is believed to contain the body of a fallen prince and my money is on Aethelhiem, buried where he fell. Some sources reveal there are two Viking chiefs alongside the prince.

The Vikings pushed their way as far as Oxford where they camped for the winter before being forced back to the coast and out to sea the following spring.

Portland Harbour is one of the largest man-made harbours in the world, constructed between 1849 and 1872 during the Admiralty defence works which took over a large portion of the island. The stone used for the Breakwater mostly came from the dry moat that surrounds much of the prison.

Portland opened up properly to the mainland in 1839 when the first bridge was built, replacing the need for a ferry to get onto the island.

Making your way back to Newground, past the Olympic Rings is the War Memorial, dedicated to 223 fallen heroes from the First World War and 22 from the Second World War. It was designed by two masons from Easton at a cost of £523 and erected in November 1926. Just past the memorial is Old Hill, the original path from Underhill.

Newground is an old quarry abandoned in 1837 and levelled by convicts in the 1870s to provide the soldiers from the Verne Citadel with a clear view of fire. Before the quarries moved inland with the arrival of steam power in the late 18th Century, Tophill was a land of fields and farms that fed two windmills behind Wakeham. Scattered in the landscape were many Neolithic and Bronze age stone circles and burial mounds. The biggest and most famous burial mound was the king's barrow, believed to be that of a Celtic king called Bran. It was destroyed by quarrying in the mid-19th Century just south of here in King Barrow. The area has been a nature reserve since 2004 and is well worth exploring if you have the time. A huge number of Roman artefacts were also discovered there. It is home to a wide range of plants and animals and at its most southerly edge is a fossil forest, the remains of calcified algae that grew at the base of the trees.

Carry on along Newground, towards the east of the island until just before the last parking area, to the Newground Legacy Trail Waypoint, created with others around the island during the build up to the Olympics. They represent an historic area of some of Portland's most significant landmarks.

This spiral drystone wall was built by Shaun Seaman from the Dry Stone Walling Association. Within its spiral are sculptured reliefs created by Paul Crabtree and Hannah Sofaer from the Sculpture and Quarry Trust at the Drill Hall on Easton Lane, representing the biodiversity of Portland. At its centre is a fossilized footprint of a dinosaur from a nearby quarry formed around 145 million years ago when Portland was a land mass where the Bahamas is now.

From the gap in the trees, you can see the Citadel, constructed by convicts from the prison at the Grove between 1866 and 1887 to hold 1,000 troops to protect the coast from the French. The barracks were built underground beneath vaulted brickwork, making them bombproof from shells fired from enemy ships in the Channel. In 1903, it was converted into an infantry barrack for the Royal Engineers. It had nine fixed and ten mobile artillery guns pointing in all directions. In its construction, an Iron Age hillfort was destroyed and a Neolithic dolmen was dismantled and used as a rockery in the governor's garden at the Grove prison.

In 1948, it became a prison housing category 1 convicts from Grove Prison that became a Borstal. The prison closed in 2013 to become an Immigration Removal Centre a year later, holding 580 people until it reverted to a prison in 2018 holding 500 Category C sex offenders.

Running around Verne Hill in front of the moat is the Merchants Railway, opened in 1826 to transfer stone from the inland quarries to Castletown where it would be loaded onto barges and shipped away to all corners of the world. Horses pulled the wagons until the arrival of steam engines at the tail end of the 19th Century. It closed in 1940 when it became more efficient to carry the stone on the road by traction engine.

Continuing eastwards, cross the bridge, taking note of the two other bridges below that were part of the Merchants Railway, but do not hang about because cars and vans tend to rush past without regard for pedestrians. Just past the junction of Verne Hill Road is the entrance to the High Angle Battery on the right. This defence complex, known to locals as the 'Ghost Tunnels', was built in 1892 to house 15 muzzle loaded cannons that fired a shell high into the air to land on the decks of invading ships threatening the harbour, which were by then constructed with metal hulls.

A shot was never fired in anger nor were the defences even needed as war footing with France eased by the turn of the 20th Century, becoming allies in time for the beginning of the Great War with Germany.

To the east of the defence works is Fancy's Farm where you can stop for refreshments and use the toilet. The grounds used to be MoD property until 1996, connected to the Royal Navy and the dockyard. It is now a community farm of alpacas, Portland sheep, goats and wallabies, leased from 2012 after their site in Southwell was taken away.

Entry is free, though donations are gratefully received as this is their only source of income. It lies within an area designated a Site of Special Scientific Interest (SSSI) and has rare plants and native wildlife.

From Fancy's Farm, carry on along the gravel track towards the Young Offenders Institution (YOI) that can be seen on the horizon to the south and pass through the metal gate into the old Admiralty Quarry. Over the bank on the right hand side is Waycroft Quarry, still active producing aggregate for the construction industry and in the process of being filled in.

All the land north of the Grove near to the YOI, along the east coast to Verne Hill and west of Waycroft is Admiralty Quarry, now mostly filled in apart from around Nicodemus Knob on the cliff edge. Admiralty Quarry was government owned and worked by convicts to construct the sea defences in return for an easier time when they were sent to the penal colony in Australia. Stone from here was used to build the citadel, the prison, the breakwater and St. Peter's Church.

Despite its coincidental phallic shape, the word knob in Nicodemus Knob comes from the 14th Century low German word meaning knoll or isolated hill. It can be accessed by several paths through the rocks or by an easier route from the Engine Shed just north of the YOI. Nicodemus Knob is a stone stack left over from quarrying as a sea marker. Nicodemus was a priest and early follower of Jesus who helped prepare the crucified son of God for his entombment. Nicodemus was also the first Christian martyr.

Follow the path round to the left heading towards the sea for beautiful views across Weymouth Bay of the Purbeck Hills. The building here is the old Engine Shed which used to house steam engines and store quarry equipment for Admiralty Quarries. The drystone walls in the grounds behind that were rebuilt in preparation for the Olympic sailing events in 2012. Added to them are two engraved poems from local quarryman and poet, Skylark Durston. See if you can find them. They were carved by Weymouth College stonemasonry student, Ian Chambers, and donated by Albion Stone.

Nicodemus Knob

One of the poems reads,

Time also rings the changes
the old gives way to new,
What once supported many
is now supporting few.

Old skills become redundant
eroded by machines.
And quarry bells no longer ring
except in old men's dreams.

Just a few paces southwest from here is St. Peter's 'Convict' Church, built in 1872 by the prisoners for use by them and the prison staff. It is one of the most ornate churches on Portland with fine carved pews, an open timbered ceiling of Finnish Redwood, and a beautiful mosaic floor representing the four Evangelists. The church became redundant many years ago and is now in private possession, and sadly neglected and slowly decaying. At the time of writing, Friends of St. Peter's Church are in the process of saving the important heritage site from further erosion by registering it as an Asset of Community Value.

East of the Church is the Young Offenders Institution, HM Prison, Portland. To quarry the stone to build the Citadel and sea defences, the convicts needed a prison to house them. In 1847, locals protested at the destruction of a Bronze Age stone circle to make way for the prison, but to no avail. The prison was built the following year. It was a top security jail for category one criminals who had escaped the gallows. Prisoners were transferred to the Citadel in 1948 and the prison became a Borstal for young offenders. It changed its name to the Youth Custody Centre in 1983 and the Young Offenders Institution (YOI) five years later. It holds up to 519 young men between the ages of 18 and 21.

Follow the road round to the back of the YOI and head south along the top of the cliff. Below is East Weares with much of the area to the north the property of Portland Port. See if you can spot any of the Portland goats which are used to keep the vegetation under control.

Continue on the road beside the YOI until you reach a Victorian sewage vent pipe on the left, where a signed footpath takes you down to the old railway line known as the Cuttings. This path was used to take workers to and from the waterworks that pumped water up to the prison until it was closed down in the early 1900s due to an outbreak of typhoid which killed several prisoners.

It was constructed in the late 1840s with only the reservoirs surviving today. The reservoirs were used as a swimming pool from 1926 to 1933 when it was shut down after a borstal boy drowned during a swimming event, and it fell into decay. Today it is known as tadpole pond for obvious reasons.

Below the reservoirs is the ruin of Folly Pier, an early 17th Century construction used to ship stone for the erection of Banqueting House in Whitehall, London in 1619 for James I. It was the main pier until the construction of King's Pier to the north and Durdle Pier to the south, used by Christopher Wren to rebuild London after the Great Fire of 1666, most importantly St. Paul's Cathedral and 51 churches. Folly Pier was destroyed by a great storm in 1745.

The stone building inland from the reservoirs is the disused naval firing range, which became a scheduled monument in 2015. It was built at the beginning of the 20th Century as part of naval training requirements and closed in the 1980s because of its close proximity to the public footpaths around it.

Just to the south on the shoreline are the saltpans, a Site of Special Scientific Interest. Its origins are uncertain and likely to be the work of the Saxons but could be Roman.

From here, you have a choice. If you are pushed for time or not in the best of health then I recommend you take the clifftop footpath. Continue past the YOI taking note of the large heavily weathered stones in the wall on the left. These stones are believed to be the ancient stones from the Neolithic circle that once stood where the YOI is now. Follow the road round to the right and opposite the prison entrance, on the left, is the Governors Garden. To the left of the garden is the Prison Museum, well worth a visit and was free entry the last time I was there.

Leave the garden heading down towards the sea, past another sewage vent pipe, greenhouses, the bowling green and through the kissing gate, taking you onto the clifftop path. Follow the track to a wide dirt track where you must turn left to get to The Cuttings. Keep to the left until you reach the viewing platform above Church Ope Cove.

For those more adventurous, descend the zigzag path behind the YOI, believed to be originally a smugglers path, to The Cuttings, the old railway line between Weymouth and Easton. It was built between 1862 and 1864 by the Great Western Railway and the London and South Western Railway, opening in 1865. Passenger services ended in 1952 and goods wagons in 1965. Heading south towards Church Ope Cove, look out for the 'Rock Face' in the cliff below the Governors Garden. On the seaward side, left of the old Second World War pillbox on the edge of the cliff, is Durdle Pier, where a crane stood for years until destroyed by a storm in 2015. Out to sea, the turbulent water is known as

The Race, a place where two tidal currents meet, and which has sunk many small boats in the past.

Past here, notice the many stone walls that were the boundaries of family-owned quarries that operated on the East Weares during the 17th and 18th Centuries. Follow the left path, which will take you to the viewing platform above Church Ope Cove.

Towering above you in the south is Rufus Castle, also known as Bow and Arrow Castle. What you see is the ruined keep built around 1450 by Richard, Duke of York, or possibly his mother, Cicely Neville, in her son's honour after she inherited Portland in 1461. The Castle was built without mortar, using a cyclopean method that was more common in Europe at the time, over the foundations of an earlier fort constructed by King Rufus / William II in the late 11th Century. It protected the top of the island from invaders landing in Church Ope Cove, the only safe entrance to Tophill from the sea.

John Penn, the governor of the island and grandson of William Penn who founded the state of Pennsylvania in America, acquired land south of

Rufus Castle from his good friend, George III, for a stately home, Pennsylvania Castle, which incorporated the ruins of the old castle and Portland's first parish church, St. Andrew's. This caused great friction with the locals who were banned from visiting their loved ones buried in the cemetery.

Penn finally relented after 22 years of pressure from the Court Leet, giving the locals access in 1822.

The lavish Gothic Pennsylvania Castle, designed by James Wyatt, was constructed in 1800 at a cost of £20,000, not only swallowing up the ruins of the castle and church but the road at the bottom of Wakeham was diverted and several houses demolished to accommodate his extensive gardens.

After the death of John Penn in 1834, the castle remained a private residence until 1950 when it became a hotel. In 1993, it reverted back to a private residence until 2011 when it was bought by Colonial Leisure Ltd, an Australian company that specialises in corporate events and wedding venues.

Before quarries began dropping stone into the sea along these cliffs, Church Ope Cove was a sandy beach, one of Portland's little gems. The current and tides have rounded the rocks tipped into the sea into pebbles and washed up onto the beach.

In 787, six years before the raid at Lindisfarne, three Viking ships landed on the beach for respite from a storm, believed to be on a reconnaissance mission. When a Court Leet arrived from Dorchester demanding landing taxes, he was run through with a sword before the Vikings left.

One dark night in 1960, two Russian spies landed here and were captured while trying to leave, putting the authorities onto the Portland Spy Ring. Local woman, Ethel Gee, from Hambro Road down Underhill, with her lover, Harry Houghton, had been stealing nuclear secrets from the Admiralty Underwater Weapons Establishment (North) in the naval base from the late 1950s.

I learnt of Ethel Gee and the Portland Spy Ring at school. She was known as Bunty and was a hard working Portland girl who spent much of her spare time caring for her aging parents and her aunts and uncles, leaving little time for socialising, let alone dating and finding a husband. She lived at 23 Hambro Road, leaving school at 15 to work as a filing clerk at the secretive HMS Osprey based at the Royal Navy Air Station, established in 1917 in the Dockyard.

In 1955, aged 41, Ethel Gee met handsome, divorced alcoholic Harry Houghton, nine years her senior, who started work at the secret base as an Admiralty clerk with access to very sensitive material. This intriguing older man originated from Lincoln, joined the Royal Navy at 14, soon after the Great War, which led him eventually to Portland, and like many Royal Navy sailors, he chose to remain here after serving his time on ships. He offered what Ethel Gee needed, excitement, adventure and most importantly, romance, love and marriage. They very soon became lovers.

Gee was transferred to the Admiralty Underwater Weapons Establishment (the A.U.W.E.) when it opened at Southwell in 1959, to work in the drawing office records which housed very sensitive construction drawings of ongoing projects including the new submarine HMS Dreadnought.

Houghton introduced Gee to his friend, a Canadian businessman called Gordon Lonsdale who happened to be Russian spy, Colonel Konon Molody, and the mastermind behind the Portland Spy Ring. Every Saturday, Gee would accompany Houghton to London, posing as a married couple, where they would always visit the Polish Embassy.

Their regular visits to London and the Polish Embassy, and Houghton's lavish lifestyle, far above his pay grade as a lowly clerk, caught the eye of special branch, and they were closely watched. On one of their visits in 1961, outside the Old Vic Theatre, Intelligence Officers saw Houghton and Gee hand over a bag to a man they recognised as Konon Molody, aka Gordon Lonsdale. Houghton and Gee were arrested near Waterloo Station. Houghton had pockets of bank notes and Gee's basket of innocent groceries contained a microfilm of 310 classified photographs of Admiralty documents.

Molody was traced back to a bungalow in Ruislip, the home of Helen and Peter Kroger, which was full of spy equipment and the necessary means to transmit top secret documents to Russia.

Molody was sentenced to 25 years, the Krogers 20 years each, and Houghton and Gee, both 15 years. Gee always claimed she did it only for the love of Houghton. Molody was released during a spy swap in 1964, as were the Krogers in 1969. Houghton and Gee were released in 1970 and married the following year. They lived the rest of their lives in Poole, Dorset. Ethel died in 1984 and Houghton a year later. I was two years old when they were captured, too young to remember it, but remember hearing the drama years later from my parents, aunts and uncles and grandparents who remembered it vividly. Gee was the same age as my nan and they would have gone through school together.

You are now about half way to Portland Bill.

CHURCH OPE COVE TO PORTLAND BILL

During the Olympic Games on Portland, Volunteer Coastal Rangers were trained to maintain the coastal path around Portland and Weymouth, keeping the paths clear of vegetation and litter, give out information to tourists and offer basic first aid if necessary. My patch was the coastal path between Church Ope Cove and Portland Bill and I was the eyes and ears on the ground for Dorset County Council for that stretch. After the Olympics had finished I continued my duties and took on the general maintenance of the St. Andrew's ruin as it had become neglected and overgrown over the previous few years. From the viewing platform, descend the steps down to the beach. Before reaching the bottom, at a sharp left turn, a signposted path on the right leads to the beautiful ruins of St. Andrew's, the remains of Portland's first parish church, which is tucked away in a valley between Pennsylvania Castle and Rufus Castle. It was constructed over the foundations of an earlier Saxon church.

The first part of St. Andrew's was built by the Benedictine Monks of St. Swithun's of Winchester around 1150, during the reign of King Stephen. Over the years a southern aisle and a vaulted roof was added, the north wall rebuilt to widen the church, a south porch replaced the old north door and the nave extended westwards to cater for a growing population.

Cicely Neville oversaw the construction of a bell tower and its rededication from St. Stephen's to St. Andrew's in 1475.

A landslip caused major damage in 1635 which required the construction of the Church Yard Banks to shore up the remaining cemetery and church grounds. After another major landslip in 1675, a massive buttress was needed at the end of the aisle to shore up the whole building. Another massive landslip, originating from Dunscroft Quarry to the south in 1734, devastated the church causing extensive damage to the whole building. With constant repairs needed, in 1756 it was decided to abandon the church, which was dismantled, and the stone sold to go towards the cost of a new church, St. George's, at the top of Reforne.

The then owner of Pennsylvania Castle, J. Merrick Head, was the first to excavate the site between 1880 and 1890. The ruin became a scheduled monument in 1924, and in 1951 it became a Grade II listed building.

The site was next cleared and consolidated by the Portland Field Research Group between 1968 and 1973. Further conservation and archaeological work was carried out between 1978 and 1982. After that, the site was maintained by the owners of

Pennsylvania Castle until 2011, when the new owners, Colonial Leisure Ltd refused to do so. Today it is maintained by Heritage England who took the work over from the Volunteer Coastal Ranger in 2022.

From here, you can either return to the steps to Church Ope Cove and continue on the coastal path to Portland Bill or you can follow the path up past Pennsylvania Castle to Wakeham and connect to either Walk Two to Tout Quarry or Walk Three to Easton.

At the bottom of the steps, on the beach, is a tap connected to a fresh water spring if you need to fill up your water bottle, and there is a toilet opposite.

Go back up the steps a little way to a path that goes behind the beach huts which will take you up more steps to the Southwell landslip that severely damaged St. Andrew's in 1734. Follow the meandering track along the clifftop, up some steep steps, and round to the right and up the slope taking you to the main road. Walk along the verge past Cheyne Weares car park, then, to be on the safe side, cross the road before the verge runs out by the allotments as cars fly down this road without any regard for walkers.

I must warn you of the mischievous creatures that reside in the gaps and cracks of the wall on this side of the road next to Coombefield Quarry. These elfish type fairies are known locally as Nanny Diements and are likely to cast their evil eye on anyone they consider a threat to them. If you see one, make sure you do not make eye contact or you will lose your sanity before the day is out. Some believe the Nanny Diements arrived here with the Celts, conjured up by their powerful priest kings, the Druids, while others insist they are ancient earth spirits manifested into physical form when stone began to be used to build the many Neolithic stone circles that once adorned the island.

These small folk are said to be anywhere between six inches tall and knee height to an adult. They wear green tunics and kilts with a wide black belt and white cone shaped hats with a small feather in the hat band.

When St. Andrew's Church was being refurbished in 1475 these mischievous creatures would keep moving the building materials from the site down to the beach overnight. In frustration, the local stonemasons constructed a wooden frame to house a bell knowing its sound irritated the Nanny Diements. Its continuous ringing forced them to leave the area and move out of earshot to Coombefield. The bell then became a permanent feature of the church.

There was nothing they liked more than annoying quarrymen by causing rock falls, endangering their lives and blaming it on the bunnies.

Many were driven away when they first heard the toll of the bell of the newly constructed St. George's Church in 1766, leaving Portland for the mainland. However, enough stayed to inflict madness on people walking past to this day.

If you survive the Nanny Diements, cross back to the other side of the road opposite Cheyne House and the old pumping station into a small car park and through a metal gate heading towards the cliff to Freshwater Bay. This is a favourite spot for rock climbers. The bay was once a sandy beach but is now covered by boulders from the quarry overburden, washed in by strong tides.

The first small quarry you come to on the right is Sheat Quarry, worked during the mid-20th Century but soon abandoned because of the poor quality of the stone.

Around the corner is God Nor Point and further on is Breston Quarry with jetties leading out over the cliff where overburden was dumped into the sea.

The path then descends into a dip to some concrete blocks that were the mounts of a steam-driven stone saw. Climbing up the steep slope brings you to Sand Holes, where sand was excavated and used to produce concrete for the Admiralty defence work in the late 19th Century.

Where the crane stands is Longstone Ope, so called because a tall Bronze Age megalith stood here dominating the environment for thousands of years. It was lying on its side when quarrying began in 1901 and had disappeared long before quarrying stopped at the outbreak of the Second World War.

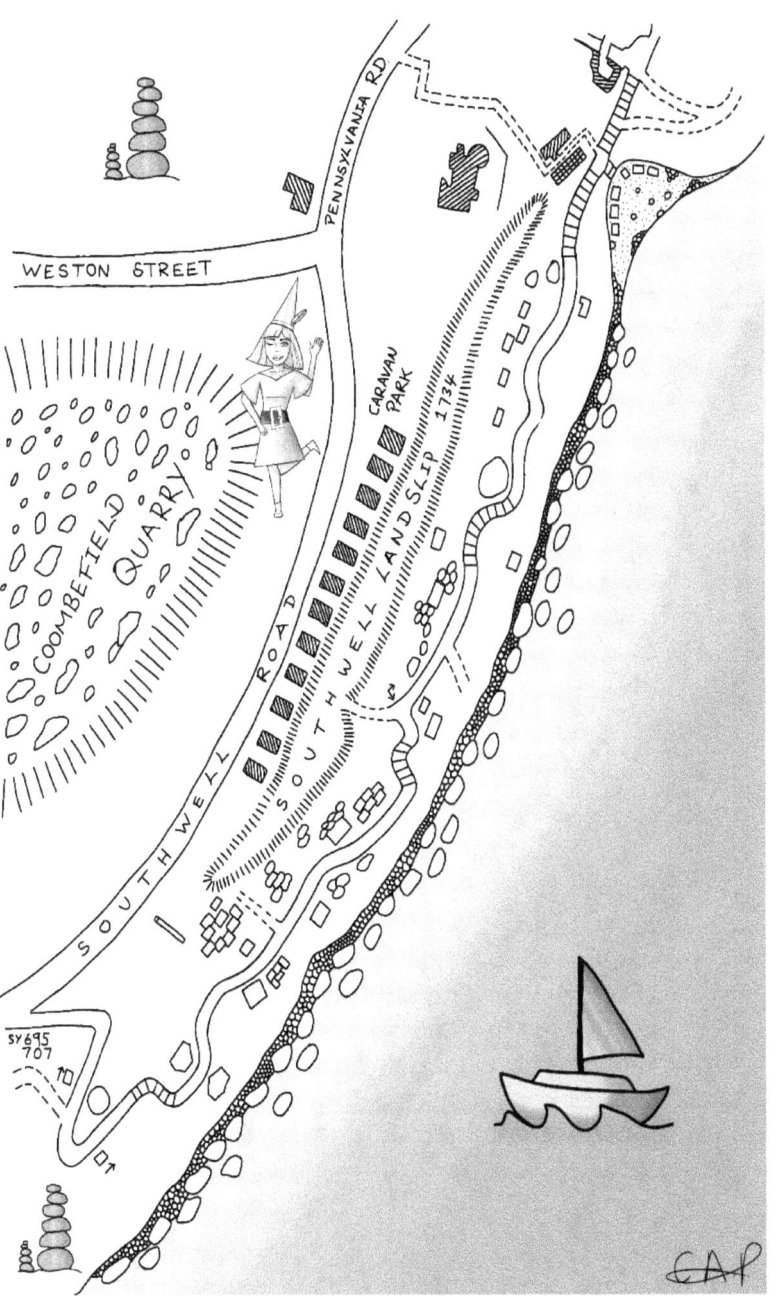

Gary Biltcliffe reveals in his interesting book, *Mysterious Portland*, that the Longstone standing stone was one point on a ley line that connected Cave Hole in the south, Avalanche Church (also known as St. Andrew's) in Southwell, the old Methodist Chapel in Weston, Gypsy Lane, St. George's Church, St. John the Baptist's Church in Fortuneswell, and across to Nothe Fort in Weymouth on a north/south axis.

Just past Longstone Ope is Culverwell stream, whose source is from an ancient spring on the other side of the Bill Road and ends at the cliff edge as a magnificent waterfall.

Evidence shows that around 10,000 years ago, people were settling on Portland. Next to Culverwell spring is the Culverwell Mesolithic Site, discovered by Susann Palmer in 1966 after a farmer's plough uncovered large amounts of mollusc shells, and excavated by volunteers over the next thirty years. The site has been dated to 8,300 years old and was, at the time, the first site in Britain to have shown evidence of a permanent settlement of Mesolithic people, about the same time that Doggerland flooded forcing the hunter-gatherers to migrate to higher ground. It was in use for around twenty years when Portland was not yet an island but was still connected to the mainland between Lyme Regis and the Purbecks. The settlement was set up next to a natural gulley which was used to throw rubbish and waste into, which would then be washed away by rainwater down the slope. The site was built over with flat slabs of stone laid over waste middens that acted as a drain forming a large floor living area that remained dry even on the rainiest of days. Between the gully and the work floor is a hollow that was used as a hearth and was shown to have been used continuously throughout the site's occupation. Evidence was found of huts or shelters in the southeast area of the site. At the southern edge, a long wall was constructed that would have acted as a windbreak.

Beneath a large triangular shaped stone, there was a stone-lined hole filled with mollusc shells containing a pierced scallop shell, a chert axe and a smooth round pebble purposely laid on its edge. Adjacent to the floor area are three shallow hollows which would have been used as hearths in addition to the main one next to the gully. These hearths were used for cooking, heating and lighting. About twenty feet east of the edge of the floor is the pit, about three feet wide and deep, dug into the stony topsoil. Around its edge, the earth is baked from the regular fires it contained. At the bottom of the pit, several large stone slabs had been placed but oddly, not fire cracked, indicating that no fires were lit directly on top of them. More than likely, parcels of food were wrapped in thick layers of leaves or seaweed, laid on top of the slabs and smaller heated stones placed over the food bundle with the fire on top making the pit a Stone Age oven.

     The site won a Pitt Rivers Award with Graham Webster Laurels for its educational value in the 2004 British Archaeology Awards. For a number of years it was maintained by the Association for Portland Archaeology who held open days during peak season until it had to be backfilled in 2022 to preserve it and avoid further deterioration by weather and wildlife activity.

According to Susann Palmer, the fields between Culverwell and the sea are potentially a very important Mesolithic site containing midden (waste) material and a large quantity of artefacts still to be discovered. Half a mammoth ivory pendant was found near the cliff edge in 1974. Throughout the whole area of this side of Southwell a very large quantity of Mesolithic stone tools was discovered during field walks. A Mesolithic habitation site next to the lower lighthouse was excavated between 1966 and 1967 after field walking revealed a huge concentration of artefacts, including a number of stone tools and a number of small shell middens, one was found with a burial consisting of bones within a semi-circular stone structure.

At the cliff edge is evidence of a raised beach of pebbles and sea shells that formed around 200,000 years ago.

Moving on towards the Bill, in a hidden dip is a blowhole above Cave Hole. It used to be called Keeve's Cave after a local smuggler used it to stash his illegal booty. I must warn you of the fearsome creature that resides in the cave known as the Roy Dog. It has been described as a large black beast the size of a man, with large fiery eyes, one green and the other red. It has, in the past, dragged unsuspecting visitors into its watery lair. In 1949, the ketch, Reliance, was wrecked here and the captain drowned. The events that led up to the disaster are captured by the survivor, Anne Davison, in her book, *Last Voyage*.

Behind the beach huts is the lower lighthouse, which has been a bird observatory and field centre since 1961. It now offers accommodation for up to 24 guests, with shared facilities.

Because of the large number of ships being wrecked off the Bill, it was decided that two lighthouses were needed: a lower one on the east side and a higher one to the west. They burned coal for light, enclosed in large glass lanterns. The lower lighthouse was rebuilt in 1789 and was 63 feet tall with a 22-inch diameter lens. The higher lighthouse was fitted with 14 oil lamps and a highly polished reflector.

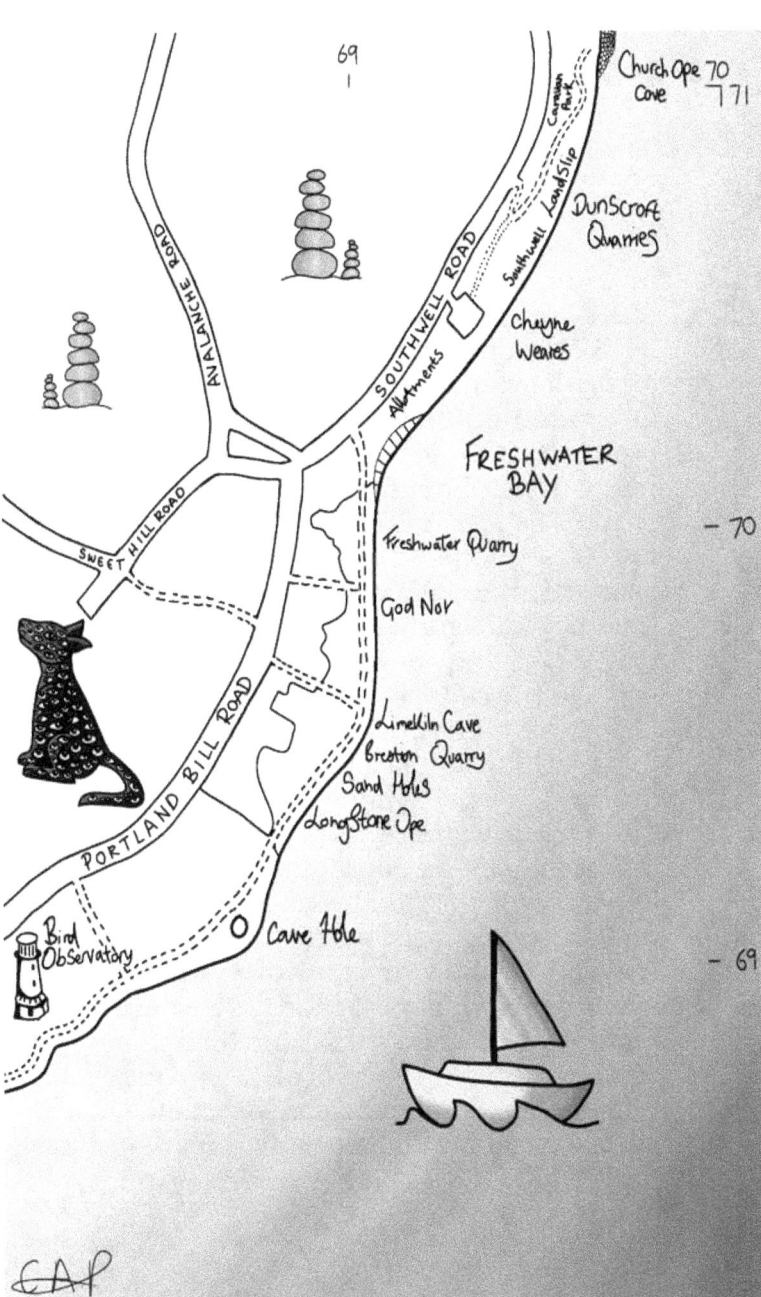

Both lighthouses were demolished and rebuilt in 1869 and are what you see today.

The main lighthouse, completed in 1906, is 136 feet high, making the other two redundant. It is a Grade II listed building and was automated in 1996. It opened as a visitor centre in 2015, and in 2019, new LED lanterns replaced the old light, reducing the range from 25 nautical miles to 18.

The lighthouses became a tourist attraction during the two world wars when the café was built and beach huts began to spring up along the cliffs.

On the seaward side, as you come to the conurbation of beach huts, is Butts Quarry. Like Longstone and Sheats Quarry, it is one of the so called 'Penny Quarries', named as such by quarrymen because they produced an inferior quality of Portland Stone.

Portland Stone was formed 145 million years ago when tiny shells known as oolites mixed with mud and sand on a shallow seabed. Pressure and heat crushed and hardened the mixture into the Jurassic rock. Beneath the shallow soil of Portland's landscape is the Top, or Skull Cap, that was formed at sea level with waves disturbing the formation leaving a hard and brittle stone which is only useful for sea defences – it is the overburden that you can see all over Portland today.

The next layer is the Roach that was formed beneath the sea and contains the fossils of ancient sea creatures like the ammonite and the famous Portland Screw. This stone gives an interesting texture to buildings whose finish does not require the clean lines of palaces or memorials. Below the Roach is the quality Whitbed for which Portland is famous. Portland Stone formed in quiet lagoon conditions, undisturbed by tides, near to where Bermuda is today, and migrated to its present position through moving tectonic plates. At the bottom lies the Base bed, a hard building stone similar to Purbeck Stone that was formed in tidal conditions.

Above Butts Quarry is the medieval archery ranges and below is Redpool. At low tide, the remains of the Danish steamer, Marguerite, which sank in 1946 can be seen just off the shore.

Further along, among the fishing huts near Red Crane is a stone building that was once a stable for the quarry horses which pulled loaded wagons on a tramway system from the quarry face to the cliff cranes, where it would be loaded onto the barges waiting below to transport it to where it was needed.

At the very tip of the Bill is the 23-foot tall white stone Trinity House obelisk, which was built in 1844 to indicate a low shelf of rock extending 100 feet south into the sea. This is now a Grade II listed building.

The earliest known name for Portland Bill is Beacon Point, after the fire beacon that stood here in the late 16th Century. It was part of an early warning system which stretched along the southern coast to Southampton and inland to London, designed to alert the capital to any invasion force sailing up the Channel. Legend has it that in 1774 Beacon Point was renamed the Beale because it reminded a traveller of a beak of a bird.

The Quarry here is Beacon Quarry, which was in use during the reign of Queen Victoria.

According to the journals of local woman, Mrs Clara Jane King Warry, during the first half of the 20th Century, Midsummer fire rituals called St. John's Fires had been performed at the Bill since the time of the Druids. Two large fires were lit close together where young adults and children would leap through the smoke and flames enacting the ancient custom to Moloch, the god of blood sacrifice. The rituals had been suspended for six years, from 1809 to 1815, when the threat of Napoleon diminished after he was defeated at Waterloo and exiled to St. Helena. The ancient fire ceremonies were stopped completely in the early part of the 20th Century because of the rough treatment of frightened children by quarrymen dragging them through the smoke and flames.

The grandmother of Clara Jane King Warry, Elizabeth Pearce (1782 – 1872), describes in her diary how stone circles and rows of stones littered Portland, especially towards Portland Bill, before quarrying destroyed them.

Around the corner from the southernmost tip is Pulpit Rock, a stack left over from Beacon Quarry to show the different layers of rock formation (like Nicodemus Knob in Admiralty Quarry). It was formed in the 1870s when a natural arch was cut away and the leaning slab was added to make it look like an open bible leaning on a pulpit.

PORTLAND BILL TO TOUT QUARRY

When you are ready and have finished exploring Portland Bill, had your ice-cream and coffee at the Lobster Pot Café and found the toilet in the car-park, make your way up the hill on the west side of the island towards the higher lighthouse at the top.

On the left is QinetiQ, an MOD site, established here in the 1960s because it is well away from stray electrical and magnetic fields that would interfere with its operations.

At the top of Branscombe Hill is the higher lighthouse, which is now a private residence. From 1923–1938 it was the home of Dr Marie Stopes, who founded London's first family clinic in 1929. Stopes also purchased and gifted Avice's Cottage to the island for Portland Museum in 1930.

Opposite is the coastguard station, established in 1899. It is a voluntary organisation relying on donations to keep a visual watch around Portland Bill. The station is equipped with state of the art technology, including an automatic identification radar for all shipping that passes, a weather monitoring system, and high-powered binoculars. In 2012, a CCTV camera was installed at the top of the modern lighthouse providing the station with a visual of the inshore passage around the tip of the island, which is a blind spot from the lookout.

Past the higher lighthouse, all the way to the Southwell Business Park, you can see great swathes of Portland which are still relatively original. The fields to your right are mainly used for keeping horses in, and meandering ancient trackways can be seen across the island towards the east side.

Southwell Business Park began life as a cold war research establishment, the Admiralty Underwater Weapons Establishment (South) – AUWE(S). The aesthetic-free building was constructed in 1959 on Barrow Hill to research enemy submarine detection and torpedo guidance systems. In 1984, it became part of the Admiralty Research Agency (ARE) and in 1991, at the end of the cold war, it became the Defence Research Agency (DRA).

When the navy left Portland in 1995, the establishment closed and the building was sold to become a business park in 1997. In 2008, a business group purchased a part of the site, setting up the Portland Spa Hotel.[1] Since then, the business has gone through a number of incarnations with new owners and different names every two years. Please see the footnote for full details. In 2023, the last set of new owners acquired the hotel renaming it The New Admiralty Hotel, closing down in 2025.

Next door to the hotel and part of the old AUWE building is the Atlantic Academy. The majority of Portland schools voted to become the Aldridge Community Academy in 2012,

---

[1] The Portland Spa Hotel went into receivership in 2010 and was taken over by Compass Point Estates. Portland (Weymouth) Ltd was formed to take over the running of the hotel renaming it the Portland Hotel.
In 2012, it changed its name to the Venue Hotel and Cliff Panoramic Restaurant. In 2014, the hotel closed down, reopening under new management in 2015 as the Ocean Hotel. In 2017 it closed down again and reopened under new management as the Maritime Hotel, which closed down in 2019. In 2020 it reopened under new management as the Admiralty Hotel. In 2023 it changed ownership again, reopening as The New Admiralty Hotel, closing down in 2025. At the time of writing, it remains closed.

receiving a £14 million grant from the government. In 2014, the Academy closed the old schools down, returning the sites back to Weymouth and Portland Council, and transferred most of the island's education to the busy business park, much to the anger of the local residents, becoming the Atlantic Academy in 2016.

Towards the end of the Business Park is a brick building with a large chimneystack which used to be the boiler house that heated up all of the AUWE. I was stationed here in 1977 as part of my apprenticeship for the Department of the Environment (DOE) in the dockyard as a mechanical fitter. I worked in the boiler house alongside my uncle, Pump. Part of my job was to maintain the network of pipes under the building, which were out of bounds to nearly everyone else who worked there.

In the fields just north of the Business Park are more Saxon field systems, now used for keeping horses. The land seaward of the horse fields used to be home to hundreds of glow worms until a powerful security night light from the Business Park shone out over the cliff and forced many of them to migrate to darker habitats.

From here up to Blacknor Fort are fields of grass and crops. Hidden from view is a recently opened mine, built to extract stone from beneath the land.

Just past the extremely deteriorated and graffitied Battery Observation Post, constructed in 1905 on the cliff edge, and the WWI gun emplacement above Mutton Cove, is Blacknor Fort, now two private residences, the Cottage and the Stables. It was also known as the West Weares Battery, constructed in 1900–02 in a commanding position overlooking Lyme Bay onto an area the locals called the 'Castles', simple earth and stone banked enclosures believed to have survived from the Iron Age. The Fort was one of several batteries built to protect Portland Harbour and had an original armament of two 6-inch BL (Breech Loaded) Mark VII guns that were replaced two years later by bigger 9.2-inch BL Mark X guns, with the smaller guns transferred to Breakwater Fort in the harbour.

With the arrival of the Great War in 1914, a further two guns were installed.[2] One was in emplacements outside of the battery to the south, in front of the observation post you passed earlier, and the second to the north that you will pass later. A BL 5-inch howitzer was later positioned outside the battery entrance.

During WWII, the fort was expanded to cater for a permanent garrison of 21 soldiers including two barracks, a dining room, washrooms, toilets, a mess hall and a cookhouse. All the comforts of home. Bren guns were mounted on the old First World War emplacements to shoot down light aircraft and a single Lewis gun replaced the former 15-pounder at the southern emplacement.

The fort was decommissioned in 1956 and sold off by the War Office. The caretaker's quarters were converted to a bungalow and garages, with the rest of the site becoming riding stables.

---

[2] A BLC (Breech Loaded Converted, incorporating a recoil and a recuperator, a hydraulic cylinder device above the barrel, returning the gun to the firing position after the recoil and a modified quicker opening breech).

Moving on, follow the path down in front of Blacknor Fort. Tread carefully, the path is close to the edge of the cliff and can be slippery in the wet and nerve-wracking when it is windy, so it is important that you keep your focus until you reach the safety of an old quarry and the northern gun emplacement.

For the next mile or so, it is just a case of following the coastal path all the way to Tout Quarry, which is now a sculpture park. Parts of the path are closed off due to unstable ground and landslip, however, detours are well signposted.

The first detour takes you round an unsafe wooden bridge over a gap in the cliff below Bowers Quarry, bringing you back on the coastal path on the other side. The path then takes you between two stone constructed stacks that used to be a bridge where rubble from the quarries was tipped over the cliff. Just past the stacks, on the right is an old quarry tool shed. From here, there is evidence of the railed track that took stone up to Priory Corner to join up with Merchants Railway taking the stone on to Castletown for shipment.

West Cliff

At the top of the hill, just past the intersecting junction from the right, leading to St. George's Church, is a second stone bridge used for dumping waste over the edge. Just past here is the second detour due to a massive landslip. Following the path upwards takes you to the southern edge of Tout Quarry and the Sculpture Park. At the top, you will find the Circle of Stones. After attending a stone carving workshop at the Drill Hall in 2001, a group of Dutch sculptors called Groep 85 hatched a plan with the Sculpture and Quarry Trust to regenerate this area. The following year the group returned to clear the area that used to be part of the local rubbish tip. They removed broken glass, bricks and old washing machines before preparing the ground with limestone to encourage native plants to grow before putting their plan into action.

Their vision was to create extinct and mythical creatures that would make up the circle around a centrepiece of a roach altar. Each artist worked on their own individual carving but the overall design is a collective effort to ensure a unified coherent construction. The group visit Portland every September for two weeks to continue their work.

The exception to the rule is the magnificent Roy Dog sculpture created in 2018 by local artist Damien Briggs, based on the hellhound of Cave Hole.

This site is also used by local witches and other pagans for rituals and ceremonies to celebrate the Wheel of the Year cycles of the eight sabbats and the full moons.

Follow the path at the top end of the Circle of Stones. Turn left, taking you into the Sculpture Park that was started up in 1983 by the Sculpture and Quarry Trust as a showcase of stone carvers from across the country.

One of the first artist to work here was Antony Gormley, the 1994 Turner Prize winner, before he became famous for his *Angel of the North* sculpture in Gateshead, Tyne and Wear and his 100 life size cast iron figures facing towards the sea on Cosby Beach in Merseyside. His *Still Falling* life-sized figure is sculpted into the rock face of a small island of unquarried land close to Wide Street.

I will leave it for you to find on your own amongst over fifty sculptures scattered around the old quarry.

Making your way northwards through the quarry, about halfway, on the left is Lano's Bridge, constructed in 1854 as part of the Merchants Railway system, carrying stone to Priory Corner pulled by horse-drawn wagons.

One sculpture that you cannot miss at the north end of the quarry is the *Serpent Steps and Alignment* by Christine Fox. Follow the body of the serpent from its tail on the path, which originally emerged from an egg that went missing at some point in the past, up a steep bank to its head at the top, gazing towards a row of standing stones on a north/south axis. It is a beautiful spot to take a rest looking down towards Underhill, Chesil Beach, Lyme Bay and Verne Common. This is my favourite place to watch the sunset.

Tout means 'lookout'. Tout Quarry was commercially worked from 1780 right up to 1982, with its last contract of 30,000 tonnes of boulders for sea defences along the coast.

The sculpture park came into operation the following year, attracting thousands of visitors to the area. In 2004, it was designated as a nature reserve and a Site of Special Scientific

Interest, and since 2012, has been under the management of the Dorset Wildlife Trust.

As part of the London 2012 Inspire Programme, Paul Crabtree and Hannah Sofaer from the Portland Sculpture and Quarry Trust conceived the *Walk Through Time* project in Tout Quarry; 140 million years experienced through art, dance and drama performed by pupils from the Royal Manor College. This quote from The Timekeeper sums up the experience beautifully.

"Portland is shaped by the elemental forces of nature and quarrying, where human time and geological time visibly intersect. The stone holds the evidence of life on earth before 'civilisation' arrived, underpinning the fragile layer of ecology on which we exist.

We have been through the Silurian Period, the Permian Period, the Triassic and Jurassic Periods, the Cretaceous and Tertiary Periods to the coming of modern man. We have arrived at an era where nature and nurture combine, where man exploits the earth's resources to create and destroy, to enrich and extinguish. We must listen to the whispers of the stone and keep in mind that once man has gone, the stones will live on."

From the quarry, you can return to Newground by turning right at the T-junction by the serpent's tail towards the tunnel under Wide Street. Turning left up the gravel path before reaching the tunnel will take you to the Memory Stones. This modern stone circle was the idea of sculptor, Hannah Sofaer, of the Portland Sculpture and Quarry Trust based in the Drill Hall on Easton Street. She selected the twelve stones from all the different quarries operating on the island. The stones are aligned to the passage of the Sun and changing seasons and make connections to the ecology, geology, art, architecture, archaeology and quarrying history of the landscape.

The site opened on the summer solstice, 21st June 2017, with a choreographed dance and sound performance by fifty students from the Isle of Portland Aldridge Community Academy.

From here, you can cross the road to get back to Newground or return to the sculpture park following the path all the way to the cliff at Priory Corner to make your way down under.

TOUT QUARRY TO CASTLETOWN

The road outside Tout Quarry is Priory Corner, which used to run close to the cliff edge. It was moved inland to its present location in 1996 because of fears of a landslip.

The refurbished crane was erected the following year to commemorate the point where Portland Stone was brought out of the quarries and transferred to the Merchants Railway to take on to Castletown.

Further down the road is the *Spirit of Portland* sculpture by Joanna Szwalska, depicting a fisherman and quarryman, representing two of the traditional industries on Portland. It was unveiled in 2000.

Midway between the two is a path leading down Lankeridge, a steep slope taking you to Chesil Cove. It can be very slippery when wet. Just past the all-weather pitch, opposite Clovens Road, on the left is a path that will take you down to the sea wall.

The new housing estate at the top of the path, overlooking the sea, was built on the site of my old junior school (Cliff School) which had been

The Alignment

constructed in 1913 for children aged eight to thirteen in the Underhill catchment. In 2012, it opted to join four other schools in the Isle of Portland Aldridge Community Academy as the Underhill Campus. In 2014, it was included in one of the Conservation Areas of Portland, presenting a 'certain architecture unity', with 'historic and community interests'. That same year the school site closed and the pupils and staff moved to the Atlantic Community Academy in the Southwell Business Park. The site was sold in 2015, against the wishes of the local council and residents, to Bayview Developments Ltd who demolished most of it in 2018 after agreeing to retain the majority of the old school building, which they converted into apartments as part of a twenty-dwelling housing estate.

The beach huts on West Weares first appeared in the early 20th Century, around the same time as those at Portland Bill. In 2001, one was sold for £10,500 which raised a few eyebrows at the time. Today you will be lucky to get any change from £50,000.

At the bottom of the path to the sea wall is the *Chiswell Earthworks*, known locally as 'Sea Waves' created by John Maine RA between 1986 and 1993 at a cost of £250,000.

Here you will also find Quiddles, a boat-shaped café built in 2007 which serves a good selection of refreshments for the weary walker and locals alike. Next door you'll find a public toilet.

The sea has always been a great enemy of the fishing village of Chiswell. The Great Storm of 1824 devastated the coastal villages across Dorset. Twenty-five islanders were killed, thirty-six houses destroyed and another hundred left uninhabitable. A number of shipwrecks occurred along the stretch of Chesil, including the 90-tonne sloop, Ebenezer, which was carried over the beach into Chiswell's main street. Calls for a sea wall to protect the village began in the 1910s and in 1931 plans were drawn up for a 1,200-foot wall. In 1942, Chiswell suffered another devastating flood with waves up to 80 feet, damaging over 100 properties.

Construction of a wall finally began in 1958 and completed in 1965 with the last phase at the southern end added to minimise further erosion to West Weares. An esplanade was laid on top allowing walkers to admire the view from firm ground.

Flooding occurred again in 1978 and 1979, prompting the council to construct a £5 million flood defence system between 1981 and 1988, which included a drainage system and a flood channel along the Beach Road. Despite this, Chiswell flooded again in 1989 and 1990 but the damage was less severe that the earlier floods. In 2004 and again in 2014, Chiswell was flooded, resulting in emergency repairs to the beach and sea wall.

The Beach Road occasionally floods when strong South Westerly winds combine with high spring tides and Portland becomes an island again.

Portland is an island with a reputation for the weird and wonderful.

So many sightings of sea creatures have been recorded around Chesil Beach over the centuries that have come to be known as the Veasta (Monster), coined by Martin Bell of Veasta Watch in 1996.

The earliest sighting was recorded in 1457, describing a mer-cock or mer-chicken. A creature was seen coming out of the sea with a crest on its head, a great red beard and legs half a yard long. It stood on the water, beckoned with its head and crowed towards the north, west and south. It was said to be the colour of a pheasant and when it had finished crowing, it vanished. In 1757, the Reverend and historian John Hutchins came across a 'mermaid' thrown by the sea onto the beach between Burton Bradstock and Swyre. It was described as being thirteen feet long, with an upper part that resembled a human and a lower part that was like a fish. The head was partly like a man and partly like a hog and its fins resembled a hand. It had forty-eight large teeth in each jaw, not unlike those in a jaw of a man.

More recently, on an evening of a full moon in 1995, a creature was spotted with a fish-like silvery white lower half and an upper body like a giant sea horse, sporting a crest of horns, estimated to be some twelve feet long. It moved in a serpentine manner in a northerly direction around forty yards off shore where it dived down and then rose up again, standing on the waves before disappearing beneath the water.

Halfway along the sea wall, across the main street to the left, is a three story building, 80 Chiswell, better known as the Slingers Restaurant. It's where my mum grew up in the 50s. It is known to be haunted. Unfortunately my mum, aunty, nan and grandad are no longer with us but two of my uncles are. Uncle Alan remembers seeing an old lady in white on the stairs. My nan told him it was someone related to the old landlord from the King's Arms a few doors up. Uncle Steven had the bedroom at the top but does not recall seeing any ghosts. He does remember when the fair was in and there was a haunted house sideshow outside with a ghostly looking thing standing on the top which he could see outside his bedroom window. That scared the life out of him.

The house has always been known as being haunted by the ghost of a barber known as Shaver Lane. He is said to have cut his own throat in the downstairs front room. Born there in 1966, a later occupant remembers his father's dog would bark at the corner of the front room.

In the early 80s, Graham Boucher purchased the property and turned downstairs into Slingers Restaurant and converted the bedrooms on the first floor into a bar. On different occasions, a number of customers in the bar had complained about being pestered or interrupted by a woman who wanted to chat with them. Each customer described the same woman but there were only two waitresses, neither fitted the description and they only served in the restaurant downstairs.

Just before Graham Boucher sold the property in the late 80s, he had a stranger in the restaurant who made him feel very uneasy. A gentleman was very insistent that there was a candlestick in the property – one of a pair. He had the other, and he wanted to purchase its twin but Graham had no knowledge of it. After some research,

Graham learnt that the pair of candlesticks were supposedly used to hold specific candles during human sacrifice rituals.

A Greek Cypriot bought Slingers and had the same complaints from customers about the chatty lady upstairs and decided to shut the bar for good.

It is generally accepted that Chesil Beach was formed 7–8,000 years ago after Portland became an island with the flooding of Doggerland. Many of the pebbles are chert and flint, which is very pale, from Bincombe and Blackdown beds near Seaton. The black ones are from the Purbeck basal and the Kimmeridge oil shale beds. The majority are quartz and chalcedony with the darker brown and beautiful reds from Budleigh's pebble beds. There is also a smattering of jasper, porphyry, moss agates and star coral if you really start looking.

According to local legend, The Devil came to the south coast to convert the people to worship him. The folk of Weymouth welcomed him with open arms but the Prince of Darkness noticed Portlanders having a good time and became angry that he could not reach them because he could not cross over flowing water. As the evening sun began to set, he scooped up handfuls of stones and threw them into the sea in frustration. He carried on throwing the stones all through the night, becoming increasingly frustrated as the moon rose overhead then disappeared over the western horizon. The Devil only stopped when the sun began to rise the following morning, and he headed back into Weymouth for breakfast, and perhaps a virgin or two, if he could find any. If he had waited a bit longer until sunlight bathed the land, The Devil would have seen that the stones he had thrown into the sea all night had made a land bridge to Portland, and he could have reached the island after all.

If the Devil had made it to Portland, no doubt he would have paid a visit to the welcoming Cove House Inn on the sea wall. This 18th Century pub, converted from an old cottage, has been Grade II listed since 1993. It began selling ale and spirits in the 1840s, serving local fishermen requiring shelter waiting for the fish to come into the cove.

The road to the south of the pub, leading to the main road, is called Big

Ope. This road, along with Little Ope, Dark Ope, Lerret Ope and my favourite, No Ope, served as outlets for water to flow between the buildings during floods and high tides.

Follow Big Ope to the main road, cross over and make your way towards Victoria Square, as far as Clements Lane on your right. The building on the corner with an outside staircase is Conjurors Lodge, an old cottage converted into a workshop dating back to the late 18th Century. It became synonymous with witchcraft in the early part of the 19th Century when a group of Methodists, accused of dabbling in the dark arts, moved their practise to the top room here.

Witchcraft has roots in Portland dating back for centuries. Legend has it that on the back of rent receipts given to the tenants of Portland on 29th September 1784 was a message that read,

> *'Witchcraft is a certain evil heart, whereby, with the assistance of the Devil, or evil spirit, some wonders may be*

> *wrought, which exceed the common apprehension of men.'*

In 1816, after being accused of witchcraft by Reverend Francis Derry, a group of fifty men and women were expelled from the Methodist Church. Charles Whittle and Robert Hind led the congregation to what was then known as the 'Long Room'. It soon became known as Conjurors Lodge, after the group, a name which has stuck to this day. The 'Conjurors' held their services here for ten years before being readmitted into the Methodist fold once Reverend Derry had moved on.

Behind Clements lane is Mound Oel's (or Howell's), the burial mound believed to be the grave of a Saxon prince, quite possibly the grave of Ealdorman Aethelhiem after his defeat against the Vikings in 840.

On the other side of Clements Lane is a walled social housing estate constructed on Bakers Ground in 2002–3. At the time of the construction of the sea defences towards the end of the 19th Century, it had been a builder's yard. In 1910, the site was bought by a family of travelling entertainers; the Ortons, who toured the country in horse-drawn caravans putting on plays with music and magic lantern shows wherever they stayed. They would arrive on Portland each year to coincide with the fair, which was always held during Guy Fawkes bonfire night. They later built a cinema on the grounds, which was a great novelty at the time. The land was left unused for the rest of the year when the Ortons were away touring.

Portland Fair can be traced back as far as at least the 13th Century when sheep and cattle were bought and sold at Fair Field at the top of Fortuneswell, opposite where the Britannia Inn is today. By the mid-19th Century, the sheep and cattle fair had become a fair of sweet stalls and peepshows and the rowdy behaviour that comes with that.

With the fair becoming larger and more popular and the rides becoming bigger and faster, in 1862, it moved to the more spacious Victoria Square. Locals could enjoy merry-go-rounds, swing-boats, a big wheel, shooting galleries, freak shows and half-naked tattooed ladies.

I still have photos from the mid-sixties showing my sister holding small monkeys. It was quite a tradition for us on November 5th, Guy Fawkes Night, with a bonfire, fireworks and the fair. By the late 1970s the tradition also included a trip to the pub.

In 2007, gridlocked traffic caused chaos getting on and off the island down through Fortuneswell. After a number of complaints, Portland Council agreed to move the fair to Weymouth, with Portland having to make do with a much smaller fair on the small field between where the twin pillars of the Golden Jubilee Gateway stands, and held during the last week of October, when more often than not, storms are lashing the island. The ancient tradition of the fair and Guy Fawkes bonfires were lost forever.

Across the road from Bakers Ground is the Walled Garden, a popular site for communal events. It began life as a pair of 17th Century cottages which were destroyed by the 'Great Storm' of 1824. In the 1970s it was the site of a toilet block and later became a council storage yard.

The garden was developed between 2004 and 2007 by the Chiswell Community Trust.

Carry on up the road to Victoria Square.

In 1865 the new railway line to Portland, which terminated at a station on the east side of the square, brought thousands of new visitors to the island. It was felt that something needed to be done to cater for them when they arrived. The owner and resident of Portland Castle, Captain Charles Augustus Manning, a magistrate originally from Ireland acquired the land, transforming it into Victoria Square in honour of Queen Victoria (1837–1901). The original development included the Royal Victoria Lodge, complete with stables and a coach house and a public house opposite which was originally called the Terminus but in 1972 changed its name to The Little Ship.

By the 1970s, the Royal Victoria Lodge had become known as the Vicky Lodge, a run-down sleazy nightclub with flats upstairs. It was popular with both locals and sailors after the pubs had closed on a Saturday.

It went into a slow decline after the navy left in 1995 and closed down as a nightclub for a while. It reopened under new management not long after the Olympic sailing had been and gone. A local rock band, The Dolmen, played on the opening night and I was invited by a friend to join her for a few drinks. We had our first kiss when we left and we are still together a decade on.

The old station was demolished in 1969 and replaced by the roundabout bringing the traffic onto Portland. Both the Victoria Lodge and The Little Ship became Grade II listed buildings in 1993.

Portland's first Masonic Lodge was built in 1878 beside Victoria Lodge. It is now a bed and breakfast called The Bunker. The Masonic Lodge was later replaced with a larger hall across the road.

A large gathering of Masons assembled on Portland for the laying of the foundation stone of the new Masonic Lodge on the 16th June 1898 and opened the following year by MP, Colonel Brymer. The hall included a cinema called The Palace on the ground floor.

The twin stone pillars standing in the field north of the roundabout are erected roughly where the railway station platforms used to be. They were carved to represent warning beacons that had been used on Portland during the 17th and 18th centuries. They were commissioned by Portland Town Council to celebrate Queen Elizabeth II's Golden Jubilee in 2002 and were intended to sit on the Portland side of Ferry Bridge acting as a gateway to the island. The pillars, donated by Portland Stone Firms, were made out of Basebed, which is a good quality stone for interiors but quickly erodes outside in the elements. The columns are from core drill bits pinned to blocks and erected by Easton Masonry.

They were funded by Freemasons and engraved at the base by John Saleman with the names of masons who were lost in the two World Wars. Unfortunately they have weathered badly and the names are illegible today.

Due to lengthy planning issues it was finally placed in its current position two years later. They were officially opened on the 12th June 2004 by Portland Mayor, Steve Flew, and

Weymouth Mayor, Doug Hollings, and attended by members of the Provincial Grand Lodge of Dorset. A time capsule is placed under the western pillar. As I understand it, from a masonic point of view, the two pillars are Boaz (In Him is Strength) on the left hand side and Jachin (He Will Establish) on the right, symbolic of the pillars at the entrance to Solomon's Temple in Jerusalem. They represent the duality of opposing forces that gives our planet life where Boaz is the feminine force of the universe, the dark (hidden), the divine (spirit) and stability. Jachin is the masculine force of the universe, the light (visible), the earthly (material) and impermanence. The 'Guardian of the Threshold' standing at the entrance between the pillars is Hegemon (Authority), the reconciler, balancing the two polarities to create harmony.

Gary Biltcliffe, in his book, *Mysterious Portland,* discovered an alignment from a point between the pillars that passes between the two Masonic Halls in Victoria Square. It runs through the United Reformed Church at the top end of Chiswell (now holiday flats), the Memory Stones at the northern end of Tout Quarry, All Saints

Church in Easton, Portland Museum at the bottom of Wakeham and St. Andrew's Church overlooking Church Ope Cove.

On examination with a compass, the pillars are laid out on a northwest-southeast alignment going through Victoria Lodge and not much else unless you consider the solstices. Looking towards Portland the pillars line up with the mid-summer sunrise (at sea level), with the mid-winter sunset behind you. More importantly, the pillars themselves line up to the mid-winter sunrise and the mid-summer sunset, something more akin to the Masonic way of thinking.

Behind Victoria Lodge, the Olympic Village now stands on the site where HMS Osprey used to be.

HMS Osprey was a land-based research centre in the dockyard that assessed the potential of anti-submarine helicopters at the start of the Cold War. This led to the creation of the RNAS in 1959, based on reclaimed marshland known as the Mere which stretched from Portland Castle to where Hamm Roundabout is today, just past the Sailing Academy.

On the 1st of May (Beltane) 1967, HMS Osprey became one of the UK's most highly classified secret locations, a Cold War Python site, part of the defence and recovery strategy for the country after a nuclear attack.

The old air station was renamed Osprey Quay in 1999 when it was taken over by the South West Regional Development Agency, which invested £500,000 to improve leisure facilities in the area which included upgrading the sports field at the Officers Field. As part of the regeneration project, the Weymouth and Portland National Sailing Academy was built, opening in 2000, holding local, national and international sailing events. By 2011, Osprey Quay had been transformed into a mixed use commercial space and had agreed to lease the Officers Field to the Olympic Games to house the competitors of the sailing event.

The Olympic Village was built as accommodation for the competitors in the 2012 sailing events. They are energy efficient, built from sustainable materials and are carbon neutral. James Bulley of the London Organisation Committee of the Olympic Games told the BBC that the athlete's village would be available for social and low cost housing for locals after the games but by 2023, they were selling for between £250,000 and over £400,000, with at least one renting as a holiday let at £229 per night with 'a magnificent view of Chesil Beach'.

The construction of the Olympic Village caused outrage among the locals who lost the Officers Field, the only flat piece of recreational ground in Underhill which had been given to the people of Portland when the Royal Naval Air Station (RNAS) closed down in 1998. Susann Palmer, the director of the Association for Portland Archaeology (APA), said the island's unique nature was being sacrificed for the development.

"Wherever you go on the island, there is development going on".

The village is built on Kimmeridge Clay and needed pylons driven deep into the ground with beams laid across to hold the houses solidly in place. As any amateur geologist knows, clay tends to shift over time and is susceptible to shrinking and swelling in constantly changing weather conditions, creating cracks in the walls of buildings. My uncle Pump, an old

Portland quarryman gave them fifty years before they start to become unstable and uninhabitable.

From Victoria Square, take the north road off the roundabout, past the Beehive café on Lerret Road and turn left on Mulberry Avenue to Portland Castle. The Tudor castle was constructed between 1539 and 1541 to guard the calm bay known as Portland Roads before the harbour was built. Henry VIII constructed the castle in conjunction with Sandsfoot Castle on the other side of the harbour.

At the beginning of the Civil War, Portland Castle was taken by the Parliamentary forces of Cromwell but recaptured in 1643 by Cavaliers disguised as roundheads, who held on to it until the end of the war, surrendering with honour in 1646.

After the Napoleonic War, the castle was disarmed in the early 1820s and leased to Rev. John Manning, who renovated and converted the castle into a private residence. After his death in 1826, his son, Captain Charles Manning, was granted the castle and he continued to develop it as a residence. When Captain Manning died in 1869, the castle returned to the ownership of the War Office.

During the First World War, it was used as an ordinance store and afterwards for military accommodation. From 1943, it accommodated both British and American personnel.

Since 1952, it has been open to the public during the peak season and is now under the care of English Heritage. It became a scheduled monument in 1981 and designated as a Grade I listed building in 1993.

From Portland Castle, make your way inland up Liberty Road to Castle Road opposite Atlantic House and turn left to the roundabout next to Osprey Leisure Centre.

Do not be alarmed if you come across a German SS officer or an American GI because there is a D-day Museum just down the road towards Portland Port, created as part of a 2015 regeneration programme for Castletown. It is dedicated to the departure of U.S. troops from here in 1944.

From the roundabout, a little way up Ayton Drive to Atlantic House, on the right is a Public Footpath going up the Merchants Railway Incline.

Prepare yourself for the climb up to Tophill.

CASTLETOWN TO NEWGROUND

A legacy trail waypoint marks the start of the Merchants Railway incline. Make your way under the bridge up the steep slope passing the old Royal Navy Officers accommodation on the left, which are still waiting for redevelopment into flats.

To overcome this steep incline a pulley system was used for the wagons bringing stone from the top of the island to the bottom. After unhitching the wagons from the horses, they were hooked onto a steel cable that was attached to an empty wagon at the bottom, letting gravity do the work. The loaded wagon would pull the empty wagon up to the top. At the bottom, the wagon was re-hitched to horses and hauled to the stone pier to be loaded onto boats.

We will be following the Merchants Railway all the way back to Newground. The railway operated for 114 years until finally closing at the start of the Second World War.

Just before you reach the very top of the incline, opposite an allotment, is a path on the left that cuts

across to a narrow tarmacked road off Verne Common Road. The track leads northwards behind Amelia Close to the Royal Navy Cemetery, a peaceful spot to rest and admire the view over Portland Harbour.

The War Office established the military cemetery in 1876 for the burial of soldiers garrisoned at the citadel directly above. Convict labour was used to level the ground and build the surrounding wall. In 1907, it was transferred into the care of the Admiralty and in 1914, was extended westwards for personnel in the armed forces. It saw a further 103 burials from the Second World War, including twelve German airmen and a Norwegian Merchant Navy seaman.

One of the 164 graves is for Leading Seaman, 23-year-old Jack Mantle, from Southampton, who was killed on 4th July 1940 during a German air raid on HMS Foylebank, which was berthed in Portland Harbour. Although mortally wounded, he continued to operate the quick firing 2-pounder 'pom-pom' gun until he collapsed and died. Jack Mantle was posthumously awarded the Victoria Cross for his actions.

The cemetery is divided into three parts, Church of England, Roman Catholic, and Non-Conformists. Today the site is owned by the Ministry of Defence and maintained by the Commonwealth War Graves Commission.

The dockyard was a thriving port employing many hundreds of locals in the 1960s and 70s. When the Breakwater was completed in 1857, it became a safe haven for Royal Navy warships and a main base for the Home Fleet. Submarines and aircraft carriers followed as the Second World War raged across half the planet.

It was a main base for the American First Army units preparing to invade Omaha Beach on D-Day in 1944.

Post-war, ships of NATO nations began using the harbour and in 1959, a naval helicopter base was constructed on reclaimed land over the Mere sands. With the arrival of the Cold War soon after the end of the Second World War, the naval base became a secret research base for anti-submarine warfare at AUWE(N), that was the centre of the Portland Spy Ring.

If it were not for the Royal Navy based on Portland, I would not be around to write this guide. My great grandfather, George Silsbury, from the Isle of Wight was a Chief Petty Officer in the Royal Navy serving on HMS Superb at the time of his marriage to Portland girl, Roseanna Banks, in 1911. They had a baby girl, Lillian, who met my grandfather, Londoner, Able Seaman Herbert Jones, who was serving on HMS Kingfisher when he married my grandmother in 1935. They had a baby girl, Shirley, who met my father, Able Seaman James Irvine, from Glasgow in 1954, who had me.

The closest I got to the Royal Navy was working in the Dockyard as an apprentice mechanical fitter with the Department of the Environment from 1976–1979. I learnt to service petrol and diesel motors for vans and boats, repair pneumatic drills, weld, and repair machine engineering and central heating. On completion of my apprenticeship, I travelled Europe with two friends, with the promise that my position would be left open for when I returned. By the time I got back, Maggie Thatcher was prime minister and had made extensive cutbacks in the dockyard, laying off many workers and my job was no longer available.

With the end of the Cold War in 1995, Portland Naval Base closed operations and the navy moved operations to Devonport in Plymouth. The harbour was sold as a private enterprise to Langham Industries which set it up as Portland Port, a thriving commercial industry that included new berths in the harbour to take in cruise liners.

It remains one of the few ports in the UK capable of hosting nuclear powered submarines for the Royal Navy.

Continuing your walk, retrace your steps back to the incline and make your way up the hill and through the tunnel under Verne Common Road which skirts past the prison's southern rampart. Continue along the Merchants Railway, taking in the wonderful views along the way.

The track swings round following the base of the rampart overlooking Tillycombe. In 1938, Portland Council demolished Tillycombe Farm to build a large housing estate of 62 council houses.

I lived in Tillycombe as a young teenager when I learnt the tale of the headless horseman who would ride past the back of Tillycombe on a full moon. I remember one evening, sitting in the long grass with a friend, seeing this ghostly apparition go past and make its way up the steps to the highest rampart around the moat and disappear. Whether it was our imagination or not, we raced home as fast as our legs would carry us, scared out of our wits.

Towering over Tillycombe are the three bridges that carried stone from the top of the island along this and a lower track to the incline. The top bridge is the one you crossed at the beginning of your walk. Many thousands of tonnes of stone passed along these tracks.

Before industrious man got the urge to conquer his surroundings, a weave of subterranean force flowed around the planet keeping the land charged and healthy with earth spirit. Oolitic limestone conducts energy and amplifies magnetic forces. Underground rivers beneath Portland created large amounts of electromagnetic power in the strata passing the energy into the stone.

Professor Philip Callahan, author of over 100 scientific papers and several books, is a leading scientist of the late 20th Century who researched the magical properties of paramagnetic rocks. He believes the ancients built their structures with stone because of its highly energised qualities, to create powerful sacred spaces. Sadly, all of these ancient sacred areas have been destroyed on Portland by extensive quarrying and Government defence works over the last few hundred years.

Carry on past the top of Tillycombe to Verne Hill Road. Once you get to the top, turn right into Newground.

WALK TWO: CHURCH OPE COVE TO TOUT QUARRY

Make your way up the hill, passing under the bridge into Rufus Castle to Portland Museum, one of the oldest houses still standing on the island, which is well worth the visit if you have time.

Explore the exhibits which include dinosaurs, fossils, shipwrecks, smuggling, witchcraft, the Nanny Diements and a Jurassic sea monster called the Veasta. If that does not whet your appetite, the coffee and cake will. The museum is comprised of two Tudor cottages joined together that were restored and given to the people of Portland by Marie Stopes for use as a museum in 1929, opened up to visitors the following year, allegedly displaying, amongst other things, a collection of condoms promoting Stopes' family planning incentive.

The museum is also known as Avice's

cottage from Thomas Hardy's classic, *The Well Beloved*.

Cross Pennsylvania Road where you will find a plaque commemorating the old 13th Century Rectory for the rectors of St. Andrew's Church. Despite what the plaque states, it actually stood behind the houses, and the ruin was demolished to make way for the railway cutting to Easton in 1901. The travel writer, John Leland, described the rectory in 1540 as 'the finest building on the island by far'. It was destroyed in the Civil War by Cromwell's Parliamentarian forces as it was the home of the parson of St. Andrew's, Dr Humphrey Henchman, a staunch Royalist and good friend of Charles I. Henchman was forced to flee the island for encouraging royalist sympathies in his sermons.

The islanders had supported the king from the start of the war in 1642. The roundheads seized control of Portland Castle and commanded the whole island in the spring of 1643. By the summer, Portland was back in the control of the King's men after they tricked their way into the castle, disguised as roundheads, and removed the enemy. Having control of the castle meant control of the Portland side of the bay across to Cromwell-controlled Weymouth. In response, Cromwell put the island under siege leaving many islanders, the pawns of war, to starve and freeze to death during the harsh cold winter. The beginning of 1644 saw heavy snow followed by weeks of freezing sleet. Any thought of fighting was dismissed and Weymouth felt safe in the knowledge their only threat was the 300 royal troops holed up in Portland Castle.

Not all of Weymouth supported the puritans. Fabian Hodder organised a group of royal sympathisers from the town to help Portland's cause. At midnight on Sunday 9th February, under cover of a dark moon and a low tide, the royal garrison, with the help of 120 Portland men, marched silently to Weymouth, joining forces with Hodder's conspirators, They wore white handkerchiefs on their arms for recognition, and used the password, 'Crabchurch'. 'Crab' for the capstan on the beach of Church Ope, used for winching boats up the beach, and 'church' for St. Andrew's, from where the plan for the attack was made.

With the help of Hodder and his men, the royalists were able to slip into the town unseen. The Parliamentarian guards were caught unawares, and before an alarm could be raised the defensive forts which ringed Weymouth and Sandsfoot Castle were taken. With both castles under royal command, 1,500 of the King's men sailed into the bay at daybreak to take the fight to the roundhead resistance, forcing many to flee across the river to Melcombe Regis, throw up barriers and wait for help to arrive.

Over the next few weeks, Portland was refreshed with much needed food and provisions, and most importantly, a doctor and many kegs of ale. Another 5,000 royal troops soon arrived from Bridport launching a full scale attack on Melcombe Regis and storming into the heart of the town. While the thick of the fighting occurred to the north of the town, 150 roundheads slipped across the river and seized back Sandsfoot Castle. Cromwell's army were ready for the attack with hidden batteries around the town, exposing the cavaliers to a savage counter attack and forcing them to flee to Wyke Regis before retreating to Dorchester. The fight was over.

A year later, on 6th April 1945, the commander of the King's Forces based on Portland, surrendered to Cromwell. The war was over for Portland but left ripe for the plundering of its stone.

Carry on past Pennsylvania Castle and follow the wide gravel path just before the new housing estate to Perryfield Quarry, owned by Portland Stone Firms. It is one of the largest quarries on Portland, switching to mining techniques in 2017.

My Uncle, Pump Saunders, started work here on his 14th birthday in 1946.

> *"We sort of had to go round with the old chap who measured the stone. He calls you the paint-pot boy and you had to paint numbers on the stone with the measurements he used to tell you. Then after that, you would go back to the quarry and do a bit of work, trying to use a kivel to square the side of the stone. A kivel was like*

a pickaxe with a point at one end and a flat edge on the other. With the point, you would pick away in what we called the run line and take it down so far, so you would get like a flat edge so you can hit it with the other end and break a piece off. All the stones had to be worked, made proper square.

After I had worked here for about a year, there was a crane down at the bottom of the quarry and the jib ran away and the crane collapsed, actually because the wooden stays on the crane were rotted and had a wire hawser up the side of the crane that went down with a piece of stone in it. Of course, it tipped over and a bloke was up top the bank right underneath the jib and he got killed. This chap they called Richard Otter. He was known as Dicky Bird because he was always whistling.

This was a railway line here. We used to bring the carriages and trucks here first for us to load the stone on. A couple of years after that they started to build a sawmill there, so we used to get the railway wagons to shunt the masonry. Just here, when I started, there used to be a crane there, a small iron crane which must have been used for people to take the rubble off by hand, pick-axe and shovel... Three or four nippers came one night and let the brakes off and pushed the carriage, they just had to move it a bit and it ran down the slope and straight into the mills.
The stone in Perryfields, this Whitbed is a marvellous stone."

Pump taps the stone with another stone.

"That is a good stone there. If it had a fault in it, it would make a more dull sound."

Follow the quarry round to the left, towards the southern windmill, one of two windmills that were first recorded in the Land Revenue Accounts of 1608 but could be over a century older. The Pearce family owned them from the 1600s up to the late 1800s, when they stopped operating and fell into deterioration due to cheap mass-produced flour and bread becoming readily available due to the island's new rail and road links from the mainland.

The southern windmill on Cotton Fields was used as a pillbox by the Home Guard in the Second World War. In the late 1980s, Portland Stone Firms, which own the land, announced they were going to demolish the windmill to get to the stone beneath using the 1952 Mining Act, giving them unlimited rights for 100 years to help rebuild bomb damaged cities after the war. A storm of protests stopped the demolition and the quarry owners agreed to cut around the windmill and maintain it.

The northern windmill is called Angel Mill and for as long as I can remember had a wooden shaft laid across its roof which was removed in 1983 and housed in the garden of the museum. Today, the windmill is in private hands with the promise that it will be renovated back to working order.

Carry on past the windmill to the end of the path, turn right, and then left past Furland's housing estate to Gypsy Lane/Providence Place. Halfway down is one of the best Tudor cottages on the island and only one of two that are thatched, the other being Portland Museum.

At the turn of the 20th Century, the son of a wealthy Portland family who owned a lot of land in and around Weston, including Gypsy Lane, joined the Methodist congregation, much to the disgust of his father who was a stout supporter of the Church of England. For fear of upsetting his Reverend, the father changed his will so the son, instead of inheriting Gypsy Lane, only got a shilling. Some time later, the son inherited the street through marriage, causing him to rejoice, "'Tis providence, 'tis providence," through Weston. Portland Council decided to rename the street

Providence Place, even though most locals today still refer to it as Gypsy Lane.

Now you are in the Victorian village of Weston which grew northwards from the ancient pond that was described as being deep with rough-hewn stone walls, steps and ramps. It was the main watering place but by the 1870s, it had become dirty with mud and was undrinkable. When a young boy drowned in it in 1902, the pond was filled in.

Weston was largely a farming village with the main farm just down the road from Gypsy Lane.

Follow the road southwards to the junction with Weston Street and cross Weston Road opposite Barnicoats footpath, next to the nursery leading to Westcliff. The small group of stones on the verge is all that is left of the pond. A small stream fed the pond from a spring that flowed from just south of St. George's Church at the top of Reforne.

From the bottom of Weston, make your way northwards, past the housing estates to the old school playing fields.

During work for an all-weather pitch in 2004, a first Century Roman building was discovered. The pitch was built in a new location to allow for a full archaeological excavation by AC Archaeology. Beneath the topsoil, they found the outline of a round stone structure with a porch, cut through on one side by a ditch full of Roman pottery. Overlaying the structure are the walls of a large building, more than 18 inches tall, thought to be most likely early Medieval. It could, perhaps be a barn or maybe a Saxon longhouse. On the southeast side of this large structure, at a lower level, are several well-tooled stones adjacent to each other, forming what is possibly an entrance to a quality building, almost certainly Roman.

Carry on walking to St. George's Church.

The Georgian Church, constructed between 1754 and 1766, was partly funded by money from the Stone Grant Fund that was started by Charles II for Portland's support to his father during the Civil War. A tax of one shilling for every tonne of stone excavated from Common land was split, with 9d going to Portland and 3d to the Crown.

Because of the precarious state of St. Andrew's after a major landslip twenty years earlier, in 1753 a committee approved of a new church designed for 600 people at the top of Reforne, using prepared plans of local architect, Thomas Gilbert, whose roots on the island were said to go back 500 years. His design for the church included a central dome, similar to Christopher Wren's design for St. Paul's Cathedral in the centre of London nearly 100 years earlier. One of his ancestors, also Thomas Gilbert, was an apprentice of Christopher Wren and a member of the London Masons Company. He became the supervisor of 'His Majesty's Quarries', supplying Portland stone to rebuild London after the Great Fire in 1666, making him the largest stone merchant on the island.

The church's name comes not only from the saint who defeated the dragon but also because George II donated the land and gave £500 towards its construction. Soon after opening, the burial ground flooded. Every inhabitant and boy on the island capable of labour were ordered to assemble at the churchyard and dig a ditch around it or face a fine of two shillings and sixpence.

The Great Storm of 1795 badly damaged the church roof, which needed replacing, and was also responsible for a number of warships being wrecked on Chesil Beach. The warships were part of a fleet of over 100 ships commanded by Admiral Christian, which had been on its way to challenge the French for dominance in the West Indies. Six ships were lost carrying hundreds of men, with only a handful surviving. Many of the dead were disfigured by the pounding waves and from being hurled onto the pebbles – bodies washed ashore for weeks. It was claimed by one survivor that callous wreckers and salvagers rescued the cargo but abandoned men to their fate. Of course, the Portland rescuers denied this.

The construction of St. John the Baptist Church in Fortuneswell in 1839, catering for the growing number of people living in Underhill, saw the attendance of St. George fall dramatically. With the Methodist Church (1906–07) and All Saints (1917) being built in Easton, the writing was on the wall for St. George's which became obsolete and fell into disrepair. It was restored in the 1960s and has been under the care of the Churches Conservation Trust since the 1970s.

It is said that some of the pews had holes drilled into the back so those Portland folk with tails could sit comfortably during the service. Unfortunately, these pews were removed and destroyed during the restoration work.

St. George's became a Grade I listed building in 1951, the graveyard wall was grade II listed in 1978, as was the lychgate entrance in 1993. The church is open to visitors during the summer periods, and is manned by volunteers.

Turn left just past the cemetery down a gravel path past Bowers Quarry, keeping to the narrow right-hand path to avoid being run over by lorries.

Bowers Quarry has been operational since the late 18th Century. It closed down for the Second World War, reopening when it was leased from the Crown Estates to Albion Stone in 1979.

My uncle Pump was working for them at the time.

> *"I was asked if I could go there, so I said yeah, I would go there. They wanted to open it up, so we got four men. We took two chaps from the dole and quarried out there. They never had any experience before but they turned out all right, they soon learnt the job, you know.*
>
> *Part of Bowers was already open, the stone was all clear. We still used plug and feathers and all that to get it out. We blasted it out with gunpowder. We got a lot of good stone, like I said, it was all clear, so we got to the stone straight away. As we got out towards the cliffs, the base bed was just a load of rubbish, about a foot high and was nothing. This was all virgin ground. We came right up to that bank there. It is where they mined it through, but at that end, it wasn't very good. It is still*

being worked, ready to go under the school playing fields there. At the moment they have planning permission to mine that field. What'll happen if they sell the ground, I don't know. After a few years, I was made up to manager and that's where I stayed until I retired in 1996."

From 2002, extraction from Bowers Quarry has been completely underground in the extreme southern end of the quarry and the High Wall Extraction on the eastern and southeast boundaries, a series of small mines which extract stone that would otherwise be wasted, that sits between the final faces of the quarry and the actual boundary of the site.

Follow the right hand path past Tods Defence on your right to join up with the coastal path of Walk One, Section 3, to Tout Quarry.

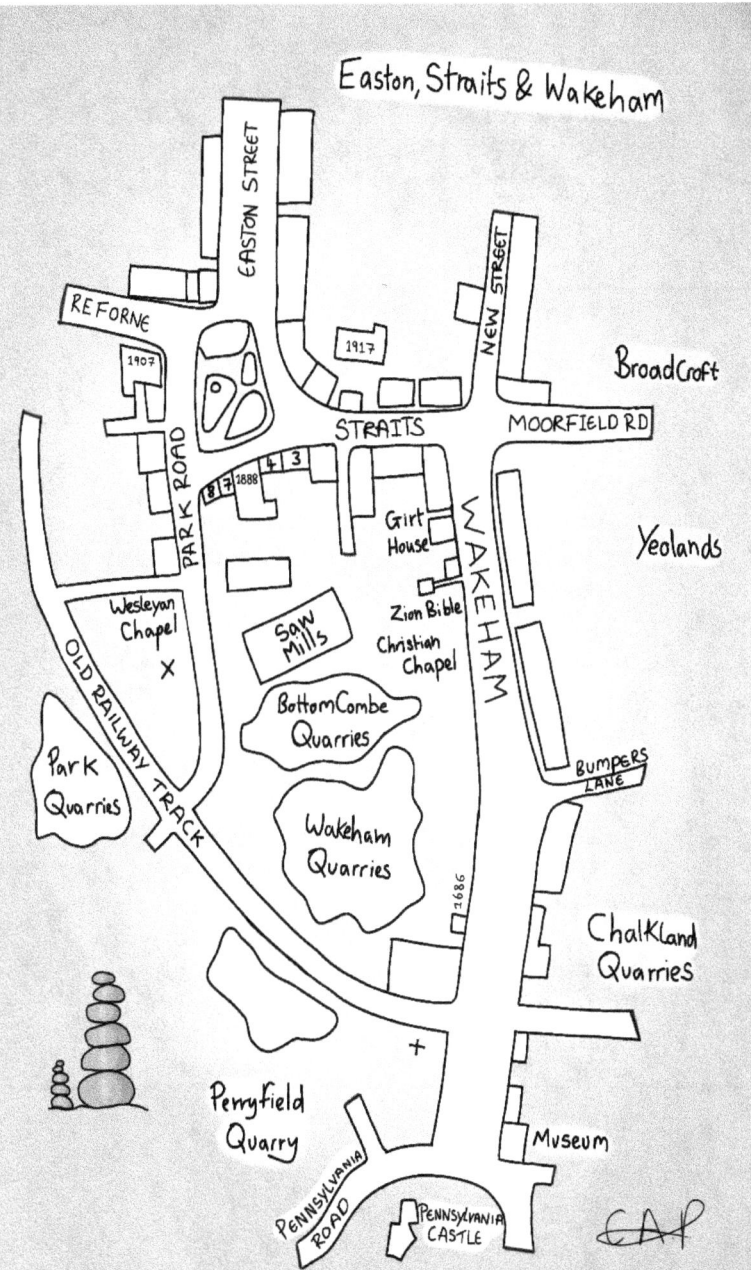

WALK THREE: CHURCH OPE COVE TO EASTON.

Follow the path under the bridge to Portland Museum at the top of the road.

Cross over the main road and make your way up Wakeham, over the bridge and past Glen caravan Site where the Russian spy, Harry Houghton, of the Portland Spy ring stayed during the Cold War until his capture in 1961.

Wakeham, the island's earliest village, running up from St. Andrew's to Easton, has a wide street due to the area between the rows of houses once being a meadow with a stream running down the middle. The village consisted of a few houses and farmsteads that used to graze their animals up and down the street.

In the field behind the caravan park is the small quarry from which the stone for the Whitehall Cenotaph in London was extracted after the First World War.

In the fields behind the houses across the road, in what was Broadcroft Quarry, now sits a housing estate. The fields were where John Penn, the founder and captain of the Portland Royal Legion of Volunteers, practiced drills at the start of the Napoleonic War (1803–1815). The Volunteers were being prepared for any invasion by the French after Britain refused to evacuate Malta in accordance with the terms of the Peace Treaty of Amiens of 1802.

With an upturn in fortune for the quarries after the Great War, what was once unspoilt Medieval field strips became a quarry, with Silklake, Shepherd's Dinner and Chalklands supplying stone for the façade of London's Regent Street and the extension to the British Museum.

Pump Saunders worked here from 1950.

> *"This is the Stonetex, where I started in 1950 when I came out of the army. We had to wheel all the chippings about 100 yards through there to put it in the hopper. We had to work twelve-hour shifts,*

six-to-six day time and six-to-six night time. It came a bit hard after being in the army. We had to wheel it all about, it was all manual, then you had to make blocks and strip down the hopper. We kept busy, we had to keep on the go all the time. We had short tea breaks. I used to sit down to eat my food but I always had too much food because before I finished I was told we had to get on working."

Opposite the Bumpers Lane Housing development where the road kinks to the left, is where Wakeham Pond once was. It supplied most of Wakeham with water until it became contaminated by mud and stone dust from the constant movement of traction engines hauling stone. This resulted in the installation of a piped water supply from the mainland in 1902.

The top half of street is mostly Georgian, joining Wakeham with Straits and Easton. One building of note is number 26 on the west side, Stonecleave, built in 1888 by wealthy quarry merchant, John Pearce.

It sits in the place of a magnificent Tudor building called Girt House, built in the 1500s which was used as the residence for the governors of Portland, including John Penn, while his castle was being built.

Shadric Stone was a canny Portlander who lived in his cottage overlooking Church Ope Cove, right where Penn wanted to build his castle, and refused to move until Penn made him an offer that he could not refuse. After a long standoff, Penn finally agreed to gift Girt House to Stone before he would move.

Continuing around the corner, past the Corner House pub is Straits, connecting Wakeham to Easton.

Numbers 15 and 17, next to Debs & Max hairdressers, were the home of William Nelson where the Reverend Charles Wesley, brother of John, preached the philosophy of the new Wesleyan/Methodism church in 1746 to the free-thinkers of the island. The twin door porches show that it was built as a single house and divided into two in the early 19th Century, when the population of Portland grew as more quarrymen arrive to work the independently owned quarries.

Opposite is the library which is built on the site of Portland's first free day school and reading room known as Maister's School, constructed around 1720 and in use until 1857.

Behind the library is All Saints Church, completed in 1917 having been started before the Great War. It was built to replace the aging St. George's Church which had become too small for the Tophill congregation.

Carry on walking into Easton.

In 1782, there were 64 houses in Easton and 47 in Wakeham. Like most Saxon settlements on the island, Easton began forming around a natural pond nearly 1,500 years ago. The pond was situated at the junction of ancient tracks from Reforne to the west, Easton Street from the north to the top of the island and Underhill, and Straits from the east that would have continued along Moorfield Road towards the cliffs. A southern track led towards fields of wheat and barley and the windmills.

A deep well was dug in 1775 south of the pond allowing water to be pumped by cranking a handle. The old well shaft is still intact with slat stone under the monument that is close to the basketball net.

Due to another war with France over the right to rule faraway lands for their resources, and the threat of an invasion by Napoleon, the Admiralty were after fit young men to be press ganged into the Royal Navy. A Royal Charter of 1453 exempted the islanders from any Admiralty business because of its Royal Manor status. The Navy Ship, Eagle, anchored in Portland Roads in 1803, near to Portland Castle. It was a clear spring morning and the heat of the sun had not yet warmed the still air as Portland woke from its slumber unaware that the Mayor of Weymouth had directed the captain of the Eagle towards Portland to find his sailors.

With 60 marines, the captain marched through Chiswell taking two men on their way to work. News quickly spread to Tophill and by the time the marines had reached Easton Centre, a large group of Portlanders were waiting for them at the pond armed with pitchforks and clubs. No one was signing up today. After a lengthy face-off, something triggered a scuffle and the captain ordered his men to open fire leaving three men dead and injuring a man and a woman who were innocent bystanders. The Portlanders scarpered in all directions. All three of the dead were married, two were quarrymen and the injured woman died in agony eight weeks later. The captain and his men were all found not guilty of murder and the case was closed. The four dead Portlanders were buried in the newly consecrated cemetery in St. George's Church at the top of Reforne.

With a new water line from Upwey in 1902, the pond and pump became redundant and the area was developed into the park you pretty much see today, which until quite recently had a bandstand.

The Methodist Church with its intricate sculptures above the entrance and inside on the pulpit, dominates the corner with Reforne. It was built in 1906, funded entirely by the folk of Portland, constructed by the builders from Plymouth as soon as they had finished the new lighthouse at the Bill. Methodism was a long way from its humblest beginnings when most meetings took place in private homes. The religion had a big influence within Portland's politics, beginning as a movement within the Church of England based on the teachings of John Wesley, who believed the Church of England lacked genuine Christian faith. Methodism revealed the 'methodical' way God works, according to an established procedure, ordered, organised or planned which, to them, meant reaching God through Jesus. Its philosophy was 'Salvation in Faith', by doing good to thy neighbours, honouring and loving God and expressing this faith in everyday actions.

WALK FOUR: EASTON TO ST. GEORGE'S CHURCH

Moving up Reforne past the Methodist Church and round the corner to Station Road, opposite the relatively new housing estate on Fancy's Close. Just before the junction is a bridge over the old railway line looking over to where Easton Station once stood.

The railway line from Victoria Square needed twelve years of blasting through solid rock to reach Easton in 1902, with the construction of the station office soon after. It allowed the train to bring passengers from the bottom of Portland in twelve cliff hugging minutes.

Unfortunately, it suffered from too many landslips and rock falls that required major repairs, causing the station to close to passengers in 1952, and finally, with Beecham's cuts, the last cargo train left here in 1965.

Carry on up Reforne and near the top on the northern side of the street, just past the YMCA, is the St. George's Heritage Centre, now a community centre offering art and craft classes, a hall for local events and an annual photographic art gallery. At the back of the building is the Heritage Centre and art studios on the western side.

It began as a national school in 1857 to accommodate 440 children until it closed in 1972, falling into disrepair until it was acquired by the Island Heritage Trust in 1982, which refurbished the building into the centre it is today.

On the other side of the road in the last row of houses is the ancient George Inn, one of Portland's oldest pubs. A year after the completion of St. George's Church, a house was built for the parish clerk.

It later became the George Inn and a regular meeting place for the Court Leet that carries on to this day.

Opposite the pub is the Red Triangle cricket pitch. After the First World War, Portland began to open up to tourism with new cafes opening up alongside spreading beach huts along the coast. A YMCA was needed for those travellers unable to afford the grand hotels or even rooms above the pubs. It was constructed on this piece of Crown Land called Jordan's Field in the evening shadow of the old church with the Red Triangle Cricket Club forming three years later.

Hidden from view, below the cricket ground, is Jordan's Mine. Jordan's Quarry is part of Inmosthay to the north and Fancy's Quarry up along Wide Street. It has been worked since the Admiralty defence work of the late 19th Century. Albion Stone leases the southern section of the quarry from the Crown Estates, purchasing the northern part of the site in 2006. To avoid disturbing the tranquillity of Sunday Cricket on a summer's afternoon on the surface, the stone is extracted by mining underneath. The mines stretch out under the northern end of the old school grounds and must be filled in before phase three of the housing development can commence. It also extends westwards under St. George's Church and cemetery, out towards Bowers Quarry, which Albion Stone also owns.

My Uncle Pump worked at Jordan's Quarry in the early 1960s.

> *"I came here in 1961. I came in November, worked a month and had a payday. Then the next month we got snowed in for six to eight weeks so we never had no money in that time ... it was hard working the quarry because the Whitbed wasn't very good at all. We used to throw most of it away you know. Yeah, a lot of it we used to throw away. We used to have to measure the bottom part of the waste because we got paid so much for shifting it because it was rubbish. Sometimes you had to bunch up the tape so that the pile would be longer than it was, but a bloke on the*

digger caught me one day. He said to one of the blokes there, 'I can see Pump down there; he's got a big handful of tape there so I shall knock a bit off this end'. Everyone used to do it. It was hard working the quarry; you couldn't earn a good payday. You could clear the flat rate and that wasn't very good!"

Pump Saunders also worked for a time at France Quarry.

"I was here for two years I think. This was where the big crusher was. That was another job with shifts six-to-six. Not very good. You are not supposed to get in the crusher but you had stones jammed in that wouldn't go down through and you had to knock them up, and the only way to do it was get in the crusher. Nobody came to check health and safety in them days, but it wasn't nice. Sometimes the other chap would be outside to book the

lorry so you was on your own, and if anything would happen you would have gone through the crusher then.

'Twas not a very good job here but at the time there wasn't a lot about. I was quite happy to have a job you know. We never got any bonus but the dumper drivers used to get a bit. They had to put in 1000 tonnes of stone through a night to get a bonus. Of course, we had to rush to get it through the crusher for their benefit, not ours."

Cross over St. George's Road towards the church. On the left is the site of my old school, Tophill Secondary Modern Senior School, that I attended between 1971 and the long hot summer of 1976. I excelled in Maths and Art, not bad at history and physics but I sucked at English. I have good memories with good friends I had many island adventures with. I was living at Southwell when I started and living in a council house on Verne Common when I left. I was caned twice by the headmaster, first by Mr (Pop) Lloyd, for burping in class and again by Mr Fletcher for skiving off school in my final year.

The school opened in 1926, taking all the senior schoolchildren on the island. It was renamed the Royal Manor Arts College after successfully gaining Art College status in 2002. Ten years later, amid all the razzmatazz of the Olympic Sailing, the school elected to merge with four other local schools to become the Isle of Portland Aldridge Community Campus. In 2016, the staff and pupils were moved to the storm-exposed Southwell Business Park, becoming the Atlantic Academy Portland, a co-educational all-through school for children ages 4–16.

After the school was moved to Southwell, the land was returned to Dorset County Council which approved the disposal of the property, along with several other assets, to the Homes Community Agency, now Home England, which in 2018 revealed plans for the school's demolition and the construction of 52 dwellings on the site. Permission was approved in 2021 by the new Dorset Council for the construction of up to 98 dwellings.

The school was demolished in 2022 to make way for a 98-apartment housing estate without provision for any new infrastructure for the extra traffic, no school places for any new children, an already short-staffed doctors and dentists and a creaking sewage system that is already at breaking point.

The next phase, at the time of writing, is for the construction of 41 dwellings on the southern end of the site with the other 57 new homes on the northern end to be completed once Albion Stone have finished their mining operations below and the mines have been back-filled with hard waste material from their quarries.

Just on the other side of the wall, before the school was built, was Reforne's natural pond that was filled in at the same time as many of the others on Portland – at the beginning of the 20th Century when it was no longer needed.

Cross the road to St. George's Church, described in the chapter Walk Two: Church Ope Cove to Tout Quarry.

WALK FIVE: EASTON TO NEWGROUND

Carry on northwards up Easton Lane, past the bus stop up to Grove Corner. This road will take you to the Young Offenders Institution and the east cliffs. The area between here and Easton Square is where Crown Farm stood before being destroyed by German bombing in the Second World War.

Continue up to the Drill Hall on the eastern side of the road.

The Drill Hall was constructed in 1868 and enlarged in 1900 for the use of the Portland Volunteer Artillery Brigade, moving from the old Maister's School in Straits. During a parade in Weymouth in 1863, the Dorset County Chronicle wrote that the Portland men were all half a head taller than the Weymouthians.

> *"Portlanders are a fine, strong and healthy race, greatly superior in ordinary stature, both in person and*

> *intelligence ... partly attributed to the fine air and comparative living".*

During the Second World War, the hall was largely used by the local Home Guard from 1941 and partly used as a community venue. After the war, the hall continued to be used by the local Territorial Army and was later acquired by the Royal Navy. The hall had a variety of other uses, including a community centre, a youth club, a dance hall and a playschool.

In 1998, Albion Stone acquired the building, using it as an office and storeroom. In 2003, Albion Stone invited the Portland Sculpture and Quarry Trust to establish themselves there. The Trust had been formed in 1983 when the Tout Quarry Sculpture Park was created. Since becoming the Drill Hall Gallery and Stone Workspace in 2009, it has hosted many community events and stone carving workshops. In 2016, the Drill Hall became a Grade II listed building. It runs an educational programme with local schools and holds a collection of archive and other items related to the stone industry.

Behind the Drill Hall is Albion Stone's Independent Quarry. This vast sprawling working quarry dominates the area north of the Grove.

My Uncle Pump worked here from the late 70s.

> *"I was here after I finished in the Dockyard in 1978, or something like that. The size of the stone was alright. Some you used to get a lot of flint in."*

On the other side of the road is Inmosthay Quarry, also owned by Albion Stone, like the other quarries in the area, worked for the past 150 or so years. My Uncle worked here, too.

> *"First of all, the crane was up the top. There was just enough land to drop the crane down over. To take the crane down took a long time, shifting it, you know. Another crew came in ... worked for a bit but they took them out as they didn't do much there at all.*

Of course, now with this modern idea, with these saws, 'tis a boring job now. That is the only hard work they do, just shift that little bit of dust. But they do get the stone out you know, 'tis coming out. They are moving pretty fast, it's so much easier; you sit down now; tedious. Plus you got nobody to talk to. When you was in the quarry years ago, you were working with a couple of hands on the stone together, you would keep working but could talk at the same time you know. Now it is boring but the pay is good. They have been on overtime since the slump has been on. They work Saturday morning. They did work an hour a night, I don't know if they still do now. Of course, that will come to an end when we alter the clocks. They can get a Sunday morning if they want."

Behind the last building on the right, the old limekiln, now a cottage, is the Fossil Forest, large rings of fossilised algae that grew around the base of trees while the trees have rotted away. Fossilised tree trunks can be found in the carpark of the Heights Hotel.

Continue up the road towards Newground. On the east side is Kingsbarrow Nature reserve. It was a working quarry during the Victorian period, closing around the same time as the Admiralty quarries opened up. During quarrying, several Roman coffins were unearthed and some pre-Roman artefacts discovered, only for most of it to be smashed up by the quarry workers, added to the rubble and tossed over the cliff at West Weares. A small number of items were rescued and are now housed across both Dorset County Museum in Dorchester, and Portland Museum.

Before you reach the Heights Hotel is the old reservoir, constructed as part of the Admiralty Works towards the end of the Victorian era in preparation for water to be piped from Upwey in 1902. It constantly leaked from the time it was built and was abandoned in the 1970s in favour of a new one across the road.

I have a vague memory from when I was about 11 or 12 when kids would swim in the reservoir and one drowned causing the council to put a roof on, around 1972.

The Heights Hotel was the dream of Ray Stone, who had a burger van in the car park at the 'Top 'o Yeates', beginning with a few rooms in 1969, expanding it over the next fifty years to the 66-bedroom building it is now. I worked there in 2013 as a maintenance person, keeping it in good running order, checking the chemicals of the outdoor swimming pool that was filled in a number of years ago, and kept an eye on the sauna and gym.

WALK SIX: CHESIL BEACH TO HALLELUJAH BAY

The sea wall was constructed between 1958 and 1965, starting a year before I was born. I spent my early years living on the High Street, opposite Mallams and the Captain's House. One of the earliest stories I remember was about the Captain's House. A naval captain had the grand house built as a wedding gift for his wife-to-be. Unfortunately, she died before the big day so the house was left unfinished until the early 21st Century.

Another story I heard more recently was that it was completed and around the time of the Conjurors Lodge forming, an alchemist lived there. A great explosion destroyed the house, blowing the roof off and the doors and windows out. Flakes of gold were discovered outwards from the house across Mallams, the High Street and much of Chiswell. The alchemist was never seen again.

My dad was working as a labourer on the sea wall when I was born. I have early memories of going to sleep to the reassuring swell of the sea up and down the beach. I spent my early years, up until I was nine, around here. One of my first adventures without grown-ups would have been Hiram's path to Hallelujah Bay. Hiram Otter was a quarryman and staunch Salvation Army disciple, built like a Mr Universe contestant. He cleared the path of large boulders rolled out over the cliff above in the 1880s. On stones at the edge of the path he carved biblical inscriptions and the first lines of some 'Salvationists' powerful hymns. When each text was finished, Otter would cry 'Hallelujah' where the small bay at the end of the path got its name.

The path has had a hammering from the sea over the past decade and parts of it have fallen away, making walking difficult.

Just past the last beach hut is Jacobs Well, renamed from Silver Well by Hiram Otter. I put some of my mum's ashes here in the spring of 2016 and always leave a carnation, her favourite flower, on the anniversary of her death. My mum was born at 80 Chiswell just before the Second World War. The village was her roots, where she always had fond memories right up to her dying day. Dad's ashes were released off Chesil Beach a decade or so earlier; reunited again after death.

Continue along the path. It becomes a little difficult in one place where erosion has taken out the steps up a steep slope but you can pull yourself up by the handrails.

You arrive at Hallelujah Bay down a slope to the beach. Opposite are steps that will take you up to Green Hump and along a higher path to Mutton Cove.

For a number of years after the Olympics, an annual pebble-stacking event took place here, until the event organisers deemed the path was too treacherous for many folk.

It is quiet here, far from the madding crowd, noisy traffic and workmen. The view is magical as the sun sweeps over the top of the island and bathes the cove in golden morning light. In the clay bank, all kinds of fossilized ammonites and oyster shells can be found.

I like to look at Portland as it was in the past when families worked the land, either growing crops or shepherding cattle and sheep on the common land before the quarrying took hold. With the fishing around the coast, a good nutritious diet could be had.

Before the bridge connected Portland to the mainland, very few visitors took the time to come here, a few merchants, travel writers and the occasional visit of royalty to rest from the hustle and bustle of governing a country.

Despite Portland getting clogged with new housing estates and swamped with too much traffic, it is still a special, sacred island if you know where to look.

Here I must leave you. I trust you will find your own way back to Chesil Beach and the sea wall. I hope you have enjoyed your guided tour of the island. There are many more secrets to be discovered, hidden gems that are not covered here, things that you will have to discover yourself off the beaten track.

PORTLAND: A ROYAL MANOR

The Royal Manor and Island of Portland, to give it its proper title, has a very rich and intriguing history. This great lump of limestone, four and a half miles long, two and a half miles wide, and 500 feet high, sits on a bank of Kimmeridge clay jutting out into the English Channel and is joined to the mainland by a great bank of pebbles.

There is evidence of Mesolithic (12,000–4,000BCE) occupation around Portland Bill, and before extensive quarrying on the top of the island, many Neolithic (4,000–2,000BCE) stone circles, dolmen and standing stones adorned the landscape. Bronze and Iron Age burial mounds of the Celts laid peacefully for nearly 2,000 years before being destroyed to get to the stone below, extracted for the construction of some of the Victorian's most impressive buildings.

Many Roman artefacts have been discovered, mainly at Weston and Verne Common, but our story really begins with the arrival of the Saxons nearly 1,500 years ago. They transformed much of Portland's landscape into field strips which fed the islanders throughout the year.

Throughout the last 1,500 years, the island of Portland has been used as a bargaining chip between royals, aristocrats, and even the church.

In the year 688, the King of Wessex, Ine, saw Portland as an important trading post, protected by high cliffs and strong tides, making it a formidable place to come to, and he declared it a Royal Manor. By 872, King Alfred was Lord of the Manor of Portland, creating the Court Leet, a court of record keeping and tax collection, which acted as a local criminal court for the punishment of minor offences. The Court still exists here today in a small capacity alongside the Crown Estate. Portland was a place for kings and their friends to recuperate and relax amongst the 'Druid' stones, throw lavish parties, and entertain guests.

Edward the Confessor, who reigned between 1042–1053, promised the Royal Estate of Portland to his prospective father-in-law, the Earl of Godwin, in exchange for his daughter's hand in marriage.

However, he reneged on this promise, instead giving it to a Benedictine order of monks in 1052 as atonement for accusing his mother, Emma of Normandy, of having an affair with Aldwin, the Bishop of Winchester. In revenge, the Earl of Godwin, who owned great swathes of Wessex, laid siege on a defenceless Portland until Edward agreed to name Godwin's son, Harold, successor to the throne. Edward later reneged on that agreement as well, promising the throne to King William the Bastard, of Normandy, in exchange for his own release after being captured while warring in France.

Upon Edward's death in 1053, Harold reached London first and claimed the English throne for himself. William arrived in force in 1066, taking the crown after defeating Harold at the Battle of Hastings. William returned Portland to a royal estate, which lasted until 1128, when the island came under the rule of the Church again, after Henry I, awarded Portland to the Bishop of Winchester, Henry of Boise, in exchange for 'arranging' the death of his brother, Rufus, King William II, in the New Forest.

Henry chose his daughter, Matilda, as his successor as she was popular with the population. The barons thought otherwise, eager for the chance of gaining new lands and estates they knew would not be granted by the Empress. They rallied together getting support from the Church who chose Matilda's cousin, Stephen, as the next King (1135–1154). Stephen was the brother of the Bishop of Winchester, Henry of Boise, and nephew of Hugh de Payens, a co-founder of the Knights Templar.

Supported by her half-brother, Robert, Earl of Gloucester, who owned much of West Cornwall, Matilda fought for the throne with raids along the south coast in 1138. Portland was pillaged, Rufus Castle captured, and the Saxon Church overlooking Church Ope destroyed. Eventually an agreement was made that on Stephen's death his successor would be Matilda's son, Henry II. Stephen's wife, also Matilda, gave large tracts of land to the Knights Templar in return for them building new churches and fortifications at ports along the south coast which could be attacked by Stephen's enemies.

In 1259, Henry III returned Portland back into royal ownership, awarding the estate to his friend, Richard de Clare, for his services fighting the Scots, Welsh, Irish and French. Three years later, De Clare was poisoned while at a party held by Piers, Earl of Saxony, the grandson of William I.

Control of Portland changed hands again in 1290 when Edward I gave it to the Bishop of Winchester, only for Edward II to return it back to the crown when he became king in 1307, then awarding the estate to Ralph de Monthmer, the Earl of Gloucester, in 1316 for his services for England.

In 1348, the Black Death reached England by a ship entering the port in Weymouth, devastating the Portland population. So much so, that three years after the plague had passed, King Edward III forbade any of the inhabitants of the island to leave their home or sell any of their crops out of the district. The King decreed,

> *"The Island of Portland has been so depopulated by the pestilence; the inhabitants*

> *remaining are not sufficiently numerous to protect it against our foreign enemies".*

In 1362, Portland was awarded to Lionel of Antwerp by the King for his services against the French. Lionel was nearly seven feet tall, a giant of a man who came to an untimely end when his father-in-law poisoned him while campaigning in Italy in 1366. On his death, the island passed down to his daughter, Philippa Mortimer, followed by her son, Roger, and his son, Edmund.

Edward IV was crowned King in 1461. He granted his mother, Cicely Neville, the estate of Portland, which she held until her death in 1484.

The first Tudor king, Henry VII, gifted Portland to his wife, Elizabeth York, the daughter of Edward IV, as a wedding gift in 1487, which began a trend of the island being gifted from a king to his wife. On her marriage to Henry VIII in 1536, Jayne Seymour received Portland amongst her wedding gifts, which included many other royal manors, forests and hunting chases across England. Her estates passed to Henry's successive wives, Catherine

Howard in 1540 and then Catherine Parr two years later until her death in 1548.

Elizabeth I awarded Portland to Henry Howman de Stanhowe for his exploits against the Spanish in 1589.

On becoming King of England in 1603, James Stuart gave Portland to his wife, Anne of Denmark. She loved dancing and putting on pageants at her royal residences. There are records of her visiting Portland on a number of occasions. She died a lonely death in 1619 aged 44. That same year, Royal Surveyor, Inigo Jones, opened up quarries on Portland using the stone to restore the old St. Paul's Cathedral and build the Banqueting Hall in London.

John Highlord, an English merchant and sheriff of London, received Portland from Charles I in 1635 before being killed at the outbreak of the Civil War. The royalist island was overrun by Parliament forces in 1644. Cromwell's men stole the bells from St. Andrew's Church and destroyed Portland's most magnificent building, the rectory at the bottom of Wakeham.

With the return of the monarchy in 1660, Charles II awarded Portland to

James Elliot for his support in the war. The king sold off the coastal tracts around the island to his wealthy friends for the quality stone used to rebuild London after the Great Fire of London. Charles II started His Majesty's Stone Grant Fund in 1665 for the support the islanders gave to his father during the Civil War. A tax of one shilling for every tonne of stone excavated from pasture land being destroyed was split, with 9d going to Portland and 3d to the crown. Any stone used by the crown was, of course, exempt from the tax. In 1669, Christopher Wren was appointed Surveyor of the Royal Works, and used around six million tonnes of Portland stone for the rebuilding of the capital.

The Tax Fund ended when the Admiralty was constructing its sea defences and opening up convict quarries of their own. The foundation stone of the Breakwater was put in place by Prince Albert in 1847, and the last stone laid by Albert Edwards, the Prince of Wales, in 1872. The citadel at the top of Verne Hill (1881) and the High Angle Battery (1892) completed the defence work, destroying the character of Portland forever.

REFERENCES

Bettey, J.H. (1970). *The Island and Royal Manor of Portland 1750-1851.* Dorset: Court Leet.

Legg, R. (1999). *Portland Encyclopaedia.* Dorset: Dorset Publishing Company.

Morris, S. (1998). *Discover Dorset – Portland.* Dorset: The Dovecote Press.

Morris, S. (1985). *Portland, An Illustrated History.* Dorset: The Dovecote Press.

Palmer, S. *Portland Archaeology Inventory of sites and finds.* Dorset: Self-published.

Woolage, R.W. (1975). *Gallats and Scafflin.* Dorset: Self-published.

Woolage, R.W. *Portland Ramblings in Verse, Tale, Poem and Folklore.* Dorset: Self-published.

facebook.com/p/Free-Portland-News-dorsetecho.co.uk

geoffkirby.co.uk

portlandhistory.co.uk

 Portland born and bred, Scott Irvine describes himself as a druid in a witch's hat. He has a wealth of knowledge about the history and lore of the Isle of Witches.

He Volunteered as a Coastal Ranger, working between Church Ope Cove and Portland Bill, from the Olympics in 2012 until the scheme was scrapped by Dorset Council in 2018.

Scott continues to give guided walks educating visitors on the island's rich history and mythology, from ancient battles between Saxons and Vikings to the more modern discovery of a Russian spy ring.

These days, when he is not walking the island, Scott spends his time pursuing writing and photography. He is the author of several published fiction and non-fiction works: three books on Goddesses, one on the serpent as an animal spirit guide, and one adventure novel set on Portland during the Iron Age.

PUBLISHED WORKS BY SCOTT IRVINE

NON-FICTION BOOKS

Ishtar and Ereshkigal: The Daughters of Sin
John Hunt Publishing/Collective Ink Books – previously Moon Books

Ereshkigal: The Dark Side of Venus
Veneficia Publications

The Magic of Serpents
John Hunt Publishing/Collective Ink Books – previously Moon Books

Kali the Destroyer
Veneficia Publications

Ancient Footsteps:
The History, Mystery and Magic
Veneficia Publications

ESSAYS

Naming the Goddess
John Hunt Publishing/Collective Ink
Books – previously Moon Books

Pagan Planet – Moon Books
John Hunt Publishing/Collective Ink
Books – previously Moon Books

Seven Ages of the Goddess
John Hunt Publishing/Collective Ink
Books – previously Moon Books

Inannanthology
Eanna Press

FICTION BOOKS

The King's Odyssey
Veneficia Publications

SHORT STORY CONTRIBUTIONS

XXII Opus Arcana
Veneficia Publications

Voices From the Ashes:
Resurrecting the Wytch
Veneficia Publications

So Do We Have a Deal
Veneficia Publications

7 Deadly Sins
Veneficia Publications

A Gateway to Summat or Other
Veneficia Publications

An Ancient Howl
Veneficia Publications

www.ingramcontent.com/pod-product-compliance
Lightning Source LLC
Chambersburg PA
CBHW052035070526
44584CB00016B/2053